■ Bicycling Magazine's ■
Mountain Biking Skills

By the Editors of *Bicycling* Magazine

Rodale Press, Emmaus, Pennsylvania

Compiled and edited by *Scott Martin*

Production editor: *Jane Sherman*
Copy editor: *Durrae Johanek*
Cover and interior design: *Lisa Farkas*
Cover photo: *T. L. Gettings*

If you have any questions or comments concerning this book, please write:
    Rodale Press
    Book Reader Service
    33 East Minor Street
    Emmaus, PA 18098

Library of Congress Cataloging-in-Publication Data

Bicycling magazine's mountain biking skills/by the editors of Bicycling
  magazine.
      p.   cm.
  ISBN 0-87857-900-1   paperback
  1. All terrain cycling.   I. Bicycling.   II. Title: Mountain Biking Skills
  GV1056.B53   1990
  796.6−dc20   89−77243
                                                   CIP

Distributed in the book trade by St. Martin's Press

  4 6 8 10 9 7 5   paperback

CONTENTS

 **Introduction**

Remember what cycling was like when you were a kid? You'd speed downhill, bomb across an empty lot, hop curbs, whiz through the woods. Bike riding meant fun, adventure, a way to explore new territory, and a chance to have a blast with your friends.

Well, now riders of all ages can recapture those good times, thanks to the invention of the mountain bike. Comfortable, easy to ride, and incredibly tough, this machine evokes those carefree days. Best of all, it opens up a whole new world of off-pavement riding. Trails and dirt roads that would damage a road bike are no problem for mountain bikes. You'll get closer to nature, see vistas invisible from the road, and escape traffic. Mountain bikes are also great for urban riding on today's rough, pothole-filled streets.

To get the most out of your mountain biking—and ensure a healthy future for the sport—we urge you to ride responsibly and obey these rules:

- Take appropriate personal safety measures, such as wearing a helmet, communicating your whereabouts, and carrying adequate supplies, including first-aid and repair kits. Never ride alone.
- When possible, obtain a travel map and brochure.
- Ride carefully, obeying all local rules of the road.
- Maintain a speed that's safe for you and others at all times.

- Yield right-of-way to other trail users. When passing, slow down and use caution. If necessary, dismount on the downhill side and wait for horses and hikers to pass.
- Stay out of wildernesses and all other areas closed to mountain bikes. It is your responsibility to learn where the boundaries are.
- Respect wildlife and livestock.
- Do not litter. Pack out what you take in—and more whenever possible.
- Respect public and private property by practicing minimum impact cycling. Get permission before traveling across private land.

This book will enhance your enjoyment of mountain biking, with tips on buying a bike, riding on trails, and making your way in the wilderness. You'll also find advice on medical matters, getting started in racing, mountain bike festivals, and much more.

Let the fun begin.

Scott Martin, Senior Editor
Bicycling Magazine

Part One
GETTING STARTED

1 GO AHEAD, GET DIRTY

When mountain bikes first appeared, their riders were often stereotyped as unwashed gonzos who disengaged their brains before bombing downhill. Conversely, this group of mud people considered traditional road riders, resplendent in their skintight, color-coordinated Lycra, to be, well, a bit much.

But times have changed. More and more cyclists are realizing that a bike's a bike, and they're riding both mountain bikes and road machines for fun and fitness. If you're wondering about the value of buying a mountain bike, consider that it's one of the best ways to improve overall riding ability.

Take bike handling. No matter how skilled you are at keeping the rubber on the pavement, there will always be challenges, whether it's lousy drivers, snarling dogs, or a slippery corner. Riding a mountain bike on dirt, snow, or grass is the best and safest way to improve balance and control. As top off-road racer Ned Overend observes, "On a mountain bike you get used to losing traction, so when you get into that situation on the road, you don't panic."

Some off-road riders develop uncanny bike-handling abilities. Tom Hayles, a Colorado cyclocross champ, says, "I've been in road races where I was able to get away just because I could slide through wet, downhill corners while everyone else was slowing down."

Surprisingly, such wizardry doesn't require much formal practice. You'll learn many of these skills by just haphazardly following off-road trails. As champion road racer Rebecca

Twigg explains, "At the Olympic training camp, our dirt rides were basically freeform. There were a lot of little roads where we chased each other around." Even if the terrain in your area isn't too demanding, simply increasing your speed will make an easy trail tougher to negotiate.

If you prefer a more formal practice course, devise a half-mile loop in a park or field that includes six or eight corners (some at the bottom of hills to increase difficulty). Route the course around trees or rocks, through mudholes, and over footbridges or logs. Then ride it fast enough to slalom past the obstacles, slide through the slippery spots, and skid around the corners.

Think you're getting good? Invite some friends and try a dirt criterium. But don't forget to wear helmets and protective clothing, including knee and elbow pads if you're really getting into it. After off-road action like this, even the tightest paceline or peloton won't seem nearly as frightening.

Muscle Makers

Mountain bike riding builds leg strength, too. Near his home in Durango, Colorado, Overend routinely climbs hills so steep that it's difficult to maintain traction. "This really helps develop my power," he says. Actually, just riding regularly through mud, snow, and grass can make anyone a feared "crank cracker."

Riding off-road also strengthens your upper body as you pull on the handlebar to conquer hills and surmount obstacles. "You build muscles in your arms and shoulders that you wouldn't road riding," says Overend. "I think these muscles help your road riding."

To derive these extra benefits and avoid injury, it is important to maintain proper riding position. If you have a road bike, your pedaling efficiency will increase and the chance of developing knee problems will be minimized if you approximate the same saddle position on your mountain bike as on your road bike. Small variations are permissible, however. For instance, Overend likes his mountain bike saddle farther back because he doesn't wear cleats. This allows him to push down on the pedals with maximum force. Dave Meyer, another Colorado cyclist who has done well in the off-road nationals, likes to position his mountain bike saddle slightly forward. This eases stress on back muscles during climbs.

While you'll have to experiment to find your ideal saddle position, it's a cardinal rule not to overgear. Plodding up hills in too high a gear will prevent you from developing valuable power, and it will probably destroy your knees. As with a road bike, choose gears for your mountain bike that are low enough to allow you to spin over the tough spots. Even strong riders in the mountain bike mecca of Crested Butte, Colorado, pack a granny chainring of 26 or 24 teeth.

Perhaps the greatest advantage to off-road riding is the variety it offers. On a mountain bike, the number of possible training routes is infinite. Dirt and gravel roads, canal banks, city parks, jogging trails—they're all open for exploration. When you become a bit jaded after six days of road work, refresh yourself with a roll in the dirt. You're even apt to make a few new friends riding off-road, although some might caution against bringing them home.

One common misconception about off-road riding has to do with safety. If you wear the proper gear and take the necessary precautions, cycling off-road is actually much less dangerous than pedaling along a city street. There are no cars and no trucks, and should you crash, the landing is much softer.

2 BUYING A MOUNTAIN BIKE

Mountain bikes don't just *look* different from road bikes— they *are* different, which means that even the most knowledgeable road cyclist isn't necessarily prepared to shop for a mountain bike.

Before you grab your checkbook and head for the bike shop, consider that there are a few things you must know in order to select the proper bike.

Frame size. For better ground clearance, the bottom

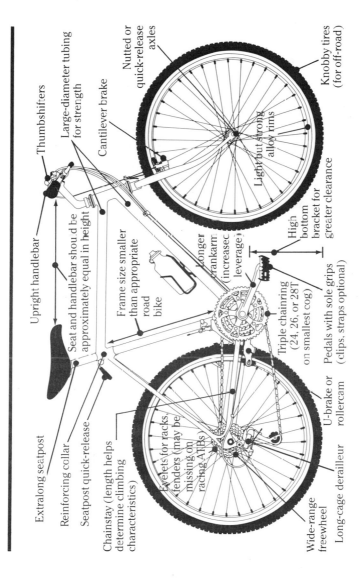

Illustration 1-1. The anatomy of a mountain bike.

Thumbshifters

Large-diameter tubing for strength

Nutted or quick-release axles

Cantilever brake

Upright handlebar

Knobby tires (for off-road)

Seat and handlebar should be approximately equal in height

Frame size smaller than appropriate road bike

Light but strong alloy rims

Longer crankarm (increased leverage)

High bottom bracket for greater clearance

Triple chainring (24, 26, or 28T on smallest cog)

Pedals with sole grips (clips, straps optional)

Extralong seatpost

Reinforcing collar

Seatpost quick-release

Chainstay (length helps determine climbing characteristics)

Eyelets for racks, fenders (may be missing on racing ATBs)

U-brake or rollercam

Wide-range freewheel

Long-cage derailleur

bracket on a mountain bike is an inch or more higher than on a road bike. This, plus the need for greater crotch clearance when off-road riding, means you need a mountain bike with a frame size 3 to 4 inches smaller than that of a properly fitted road bike. (The frame size is measured along the seat tube.)

If you're unsure about the exact frame size, opt for the smaller one. Thanks to extralong seatposts, you'll still be able to achieve your optimum pedaling height. Plus, the lower the top tube, the farther you'll be able to drop your seat (using the quick-release mechanism) for extra stability on treacherous descents.

Handlebar reach. The rules normally used to determine ideal top tube and stem length for road bikes don't apply to mountain bikes. In fact, for a given frame size, the distance between seat and handlebar can vary by an inch or more between models.

While there is no consensus, race-oriented bikes generally stretch out the rider more than leisurely designs. The only way to find your ideal reach, however, is by experimenting with different models. As with drop-bar road bikes, substituting a longer or shorter stem can help fine-tune reach. If the bike in question uses one-piece, triangulated Bullmoose-type bars, replace the whole unit with a separate bar and stem.

Riding position can also be modified by adjusting the stem up or down or changing to a handlebar that sweeps farther back. Shortening wide bars with a hacksaw or pipe cutter can make a mountain bike more comfortable, too. We've seen bars on some production mountain bikes as wide as 32 inches, which results in a rather unusual riding position. Find your ideal width by gradually moving your hands closer together while riding. Many off-road experts prefer bars with 21- to 24-inch widths.

Frame geometry. There's little agreement among mountain bike manufacturers as to the best frame angles, so expect to see many different designs. But, as is true with road bikes, the most agile mountain bikes have short wheelbases (around 42 inches), short chainstays (17 inches or less), and steep head tube angles (70 to 72 degrees).

Such a configuration aids climbing by positioning the rider more directly over the rear wheel (improving traction), and providing responsive steering at slow climbing speeds.

Often, the best-climbing mountain bikes are racing models with ultratight, sub–17-inch chainstays. Their only drawback is that such a tight rear end may not provide enough clearance for wide 2.125-inch tires. This is why some racing models come with narrow rubber. Check the clearance of the tires you plan to use, front and rear, before deciding.

Some sport mountain bikes (typified by the early model Stumpjumper) feature longer chainstays (up to 18.5 inches), a stretched out 43- to 44-inch wheelbase, and a more slack 68- or 69-degree head angle. These bikes are more stable on fast descents and more comfortable on bumpy roads, but less agile.

Our advice? Try riding both extremes to see which you prefer. If neither is to your liking, split the difference with a bike having 17-inch chainstays, a 70-degree head angle, and a 42.5-inch wheelbase. These approximate the specs for the typical sport mountain bike.

A mountain bike's seat tube angle has little effect on handling or rider comfort, but it does affect pedaling efficiency. The theory behind the shallow 68- to 70-degree angles found on some mountain bikes is that mountain bikers pedal more slowly and powerfully than roadies. Allowing them to sit farther back in the so-called power position facilitates this.

While such a configuration is well suited for steep climbs, it forces the rider to perch uncomfortably on the saddle nose when spinning. Most mountain bike designers now agree that the seat tube angle that works best approximates that of a road bike.

Crankarm length. Because the terrain is often steep and the cadence slow, an off-road cyclist needs longer crankarms. For instance, the midsize rider who turns 170mm cranks on a 21- to 23-inch road bike will find 175mm cranks on most 19- to 20-inch ATBs. Big riders who require a 22-inch or larger mountain bike can easily use 180mm cranks, although few bikes come with this size.

Form Follows Function

With that out of the way, it's shopping time. The bike you buy should be suited for the way you plan to use it. Just as with road bikes, most mountain bikes are designed with a specific purpose in mind—general sport riding, off-road racing, expedition touring, or center-city commuting.

Even so, there's much more crossover among mountain bikes than there is with road bikes. Thus, a single off-road model can play a variety of roles, especially if it's a sport bike. This general-purpose machine, which comprises the bulk of the mountain bike market, is the practical choice for virtually all first-time off-roadies.

Most quality mountain bike frames are made of chrome-moly steel or (increasingly) aluminum. With either material, the tubing will likely be of a larger diameter than the typical road frame. This is done for added strength. Among steel road bikes, the lug work is an indicator of quality, but most mountain bikes are built without lugs, using either TIG (tungsten inert gas) welds or fillet brazing. If done correctly, each of these methods results in a strong frame. On some high-quality, fillet-brazed bikes, seams are not even visible.

Whatever the price, your mountain bike will likely come with smooth-working derailleurs and brakes, thanks to advances in component technology. Most current models feature index shifting, a godsend for new riders short on technique and a help for any level of rider. As for brakes, some city models may still employ sidepulls, but most serious off-road machines use cantilevers. When properly adjusted, they are capable of locking a wheel with a two-finger squeeze.

If you want to use toe clips and straps—and many riders would say you should—look for pedals that will accept them. Most mountain bike pedals have gripping surfaces on both sides, allowing you to maneuver over tricky spots with the clips hanging down and your feet ready to dab.

Sealed bearings in hubs, pedals, bottom brackets, and headsets have become common, even in less expensive mountain bikes. They simplify maintenance and protect against the ravages of dirt, mud, and creek crossings. Bolt-on hub axles, once considered necessary, have largely been replaced by the more convenient quick-release type, which has proven its strength in off-road racing.

Also important is tire choice. Full knobbies work best in the dirt but buzz annoyingly on pavement. By contrast, all-purpose tires grip well in the dirt yet provide a quiet ride on the road. Contrary to popular belief, *all* mountain bike tires, from skinny 1.4-inch road rubber to the obese 2.125s, will seat on *all* mountain bike rims. In fact, using fat tires on narrow rims makes the tire profile more round, thus increasing flotation and rim protection. Be careful, though, if you use narrow 1.5- to 1.75-inch tires on the widest rims. With more of the tire tucked beneath the rim flanges, there's less to absorb shock. While such a combination works okay on the road, it isn't recommended for rough terrain.

Whatever Purpose You Have in Mind

Touring bikes are a subcategory of sport mountain bikes. The exact frame geometry is less important than the bike's sturdiness and its ability to handle a heavy load. The ideal mountain bike for extended touring has chainstays that are long enough to allow the rider's heels to clear the rear panniers. Braze-on mounts for front and rear racks are a convenience, but their absence shouldn't eliminate a bike from consideration, since clamp-on racks are available. Although low-mount front racks are usually desirable because of their stability, such positioning on rugged terrain may result in the front bags scraping rocks or brush. Braze-ons for multiple water bottle cages are also important for long tours.

Although few production mountain bikes come with drop handlebars, some off-road tourists prefer them. They cite a more efficient riding posture and a greater variety of hand positions. Retrofitting drop bars requires using a taller stem that has less forward extension. A few mountain bike manufacturers use a smaller 0.833-inch diameter steerer tube that won't accept a standard 22.2mm stem. Nitto offers an inexpensive high-rise "Technomics" stem in both steerer sizes.

Around-town mountain bikes are really emasculated mountain bikes. Although they're strong enough to hop curbs, they lack aggressive knobby tires, extra-stout tubing, and heavy-duty componentry common on the true dirt machines. Many city mountain bikes offer only 10 or 12 gears instead of the usual 15 or 18 on off-road bikes. But unless you commute in hilly San Francisco, this isn't a drawback. It's the upright riding position and comfort that are most important.

Although any off-road bike, save a fancy racing model that lacks fender and rack attachments, will perform well downtown, a specially designed city mountain bike is your best value. They are usually inexpensive, and some well-made models even have a lower bottom bracket so you won't have to stretch as far to put a foot down at stoplights.

Finally, there's the racing mountain bike—the thorough-bred of the off-road stable. Like its road racing cousin, the off-road racer is typically lighter, quicker handling, and some-what more fragile than a general-purpose bike. Pedals fitted with toe clips and straps, a relatively close-ratio freewheel, and the lack of rack or fender eyelets are tipoffs that it's intended for racing.

As with other off-road bikes, frame angles vary among manufacturers. Some are laid-back for downhill stability, while others are steep for instant responsiveness in tight quarters. These upright bikes require more rider skill on descents, but they climb like the dickens.

Since many racers acquire a new frame every season, tubing is often light gauge, favoring performance over durability. Wheels are also expendable, and some of the lightest moun-tain bike rims and tires rival the weight of sturdy road equipment, with 32- or even 28-spoke wheels available. All this pound-shedding makes for a quick, responsive, and expensive bike. While everyone should have the pleasure of riding an aggres-sive, 25-pound racing mountain bike at least once, few first-time buyers can justify the hefty price. Nevertheless, once you've raced the wind on a thoroughbred, it's tough to climb back on an old plowhorse. And that's precisely why there are a lot more hot racing mountain bikes out there than there are off-road racers.

■3■ FAT-TIRE THERAPY

There are days when you can't clean certain trails no matter what you do. On other days you slide through fast and steady, never hesitating. All else being equal, what's the difference? Attitude. It influences performance more than any other factor. The question is, how to activate this circuit.

Changing your mental state can begin with your physical state; specifically, your position on the bike, which is governed by the placement of the saddle relative to the pedals, the stem rise and extension, and the distance and width of the handlebar. The brake levers and thumb shifters should be right under your hands. If the bike isn't dialed in, your riding will be tentative when it ought to be bold. But if you climb on and think, "Yeah, this is how it's supposed to feel!" then even if your mental state is twisted when you get to the backcountry, it won't be for long. Just being there on a bike that feels right assures it.

The ideal rider position is, to borrow a term from the martial arts, the stance of the "warrior," modified for mountain bikes. Hands are low and away from the body, hips are over the bottom bracket and driving, the head is up while the eyes scan the ground, and weight rests lightly on the balls of the feet.

This position lets your torso float quietly over the bike while your ankles, knees, hips, fingers, wrists, and arms absorb the shock. Hand position is critical, and that means a flat bar. Drops are designed to help the rider tuck the body in for a tighter aerodynamic profile, but aerodynamics play virtually no part in singletracking, not when 5 to 10 mph average speeds are common. Singletracking and biking through technical passages requires lots of bike movement, subtle fore-and-aft weight shift, and a quiet torso. For that, a flat bar with palms almost perpendicular to the line of movement is best. The position opens the chest while leaving the shoulders and arms unrestricted. Weight is borne lightly on the hands and feet, able to be shifted instantly and smoothly according to the terrain.

Riding in this position seems to throw on a mental circuit breaker. Think of it as the "Teddy Roosevelt" switch. When it's thrown, you charge forward with bugles blaring. When it's off, you run out of gas before you even start. If the bike you're riding doesn't put you in a warrior's stance, if your hands are too high or the saddle is too far back, the circuit never gets tripped. Imagine a shortstop leaning back on his heels when the ball is hit toward him, versus a shortstop balanced on the balls of his feet. That's the difference between proper and improper position on your bike.

The idea is to let the bike move underneath you instead of you moving over it. Your torso is solidly balanced on the four points of your hands and feet; it just floats over the moving top tube. As long as the resultant force vector of your center of mass is directed downward in line with the tires' contact points, you're in balance. If it isn't, you'll topple to one side or the other.

This is where mountain biking becomes so exciting and dynamic. By creating an internal tension in your muscle structure, you can turn your body into a semirigid unit hovering over the tires' contact points. The frame and handlebar become the intervening structure upon which you balance. Through physics, it's possible to project exactly where a nonmoving rider's vector force would hit the ground between the front and rear tire contact points. That area is relatively constant no matter what the speed or terrain, shifting only in response to traction and carving needs. As long as the rider's center of mass remains over that theoretical area, he or she will be in balance even if the bike itself is leaning. The warrior stance ensures that your center of mass will remain over the line linking the tire contact points. That in itself stimulates a positive, even aggressive, attitude.

But there's more to creating a positive attitude: You have to be prepared. If you're worried about some component failing and are alone in the backcountry without a tool kit or tire patch kit, your focus will be diluted. You'll ride defensively, watching out for anything that could bring your bike to a halt. But if you know you're prepared for almost any eventuality and fully capable of dealing with those you're not prepared for, you're free to go where you want. There's nothing for your brain to grab hold of to thwart your switching into hyperspeed. You still might not succeed, but it won't be for lack of preparation.

Even having the right clothes can make all the difference in your attitude. It's important to be comfortable. If you feel like a geek, if you're embarrassed to have on tight shorts, or if your shoes don't fit, you'll dull the edges of your focus. But if all the pieces are in place, you'll "hammer." It might take a few miles of riding before the circuit flips on, but inevitably it will.

You'll cruise home feeling tall, with a fine attitude toward life. You may not have cleaned certain sections, but it won't matter. You'll feel good, and that's what the ride was for—to change your attitude.

A fine mountain bike might seem expensive to some, but it's a lot cheaper than other forms of therapy and definitely a lot more fun. Your mountain bike can be the ultimate attitude adjuster.

4 DIRTY DRESSING

Becoming a mountain biker starts with how you dress. Riding in blue jeans and sneakers makes no more sense than playing golf in a rubber diving suit. True, fine riders can clean the gnarliest trails wearing jeans and sandals, but they've already mastered the sport. Their dress has little effect on their attitude, hence it has little effect on their performance. Nevertheless, there are solid reasons why most experienced riders wear bike clothing. These reasons are even more valid for the novice.

We're not just talking fashion here. Beneath the glamour, even the wildest cycling clothing serves a purpose: to increase comfort, help regulate body temperature, and cushion a fall.

Bike shorts are made from elastic matcrials that won't bunch up as you slide in the saddle. Seams are carefully placed to minimize chafing, and padding in the crotch limits soreness. In cold weather, wear tights that insulate.

Bike shoes provide superior purchase on pedals, minimize pressure on the balls of the feet, and increase pedaling efficiency. (Running shoes, designed to cushion shock, are notorious for absorbing pedaling force and are guaranteed to make your arches ache after an hour of riding.) Cycling gloves pad the palms, prevent blisters, and protect your hands in a fall as you brace yourself with outstretched arms.

What you wear above the waist is optional. Cycling jerseys aren't mandatory, but they do absorb perspiration and have elastic rear pockets to hold such things as food and a spare tube. Layer your clothing so you can shed or add garments to adjust body temperature. Clothing for mountaineering and skiing is often fine for riding, but you can't go wrong by using clothes made expressly for mountain biking.

There's another, perhaps more important reason for wearing bike clothing: attitude. If you look like a mountain biker, you'll feel like one. And how you feel will be reflected in how you ride and how well you learn.

This doesn't mean you have to dress like a pro racer, unless it suits your style. If so, then by all means take it to the max with all the flash you can muster. But if you're conservative, you can choose basic black-on-black attire that has the same performance benefits.

Whatever you select, comfort is imperative. If tight clothing makes you feel like the Michelin man, try a looser look. For example, there are excellent touring shorts that look like walking shorts, as well as baggy shorts lined with Lycra.

5 TOOL TALK

Learning to carry a tool kit sometimes requires a long walk home. When you're 10 miles from civilization with a broken chain but no chain tool, you're faced with a long, painful push. Next time you won't even take a short jaunt without tools.

What follows are descriptions of various tool kits, ranging from a small and light kit meant for short rides and racing to an expedition kit with tools and parts to handle virtually anything mechanical.

One commercial kit fits inside a tire patch box and includes, with patches and glue, a set of 4, 5, and 6mm Allen wrenches, two custom screwdrivers (a no. 1 Phillips and no. 1 flat), and a modified chain tool. Also included are a 4-inch Crescent wrench with ⅝-inch jaw capacity and two nylon tire irons. Add a spoke wrench and you have a small, lightweight (12-ounce) tool kit.

Larger tool kits are available, but none for mountain biking's special demands. By adding items, you can bring one up to expedition quality.

One such kit contains a 6-inch Crescent wrench, three steel tire levers, a "third-hand" brake tool, two four-way cone wrenches (12-13mm, 14-15mm), three Allen wrenches (4, 5, 6mm), and no. 1 flat- and Phillips-head screwdrivers. Missing is a chain tool (a must in the backcountry) and a spoke wrench. You can replace the three steel levers with two lighter nylon ones.

Yet another such kit contains a 6-inch Crescent wrench, multisize spoke wrench, chain tool, two four-way cone wrenches (12-13mm, 14-15mm), three Allen wrenches (4, 5, 6mm), third-hand tool, tire pressure gauge, no. 1 flat- and Phillips-head screwdrivers, and two alloy tire levers.

Assembling Your Own Kit

To carry the tools, a good choice is a seat pack. Even the best packs wear through at the seatpost junction. One remedy is to stuff a small rag into the pack before putting in the tools. Running a toe strap around the pack and through the seat rails provides additional support.

You can buy tools and parts for your expedition kit at pro bike shops or hardware stores.

The following tools and parts should fill your expeditionary needs. (The total weight is about 2½ to 3 pounds.)

- Two nylon tire levers
- Spare tube with correct valve
- 2-ounce squeeze bottle of spray lubricant
- Folding Allen wrench set (2, 2.5, 3, 4, 5, 6mm)
- 4-inch Crescent wrench
- Multisize spoke wrench
- Two four-way cone wrenches (12-13, 14-15mm)
- Chain tool
- 30mm headset wrench
- 4-inch cable-snip pliers
- Two spare cables (one gear, one brake)
- Patch kit
- Three or four spare cables and nipples, correct size
- Tire boot (old tubular tire cut into 3×3-inch square)

- Four spare chain links
- Pump adapter, Presta or Schrader
- Quickfil air cartridge

Keep the spare tube in an old sock to protect it from sharp tools. Also, frequently check the patch kit glue, because it dries out fast, even when capped. Use the Quickfil cartridge in case of a lost or damaged pump. The larger, 16-gm cartridge is for mountain bike tires. It fits Presta or Schrader valves, and replacements are easy to find.

Repair Techniques

The most common field repair is flat fixing. Learn how before you head to the backcountry. Read the instructions in your patch kit or talk to your local bike mechanic or to experienced mountain bikers. Use the tire boot from the tool kit to place behind punctures or slices in the sidewall or tread. It'll keep the tube from sticking out and flatting again.

To prepare for a broken spoke, attach three or four spares to the right chainstay with electrical tape. Be sure they're the right size. (The spare spokes also make an effective chainstay guard, and the tape is handy for other repairs.) When replacing spokes, use some Loc-Tite on the nipples to keep them from vibrating off. If the broken spoke is under the freewheel, you'll have to get to a bike shop; the torque of mountain biking seats the freewheel so tightly it must be removed with a vise. The popular cassette freewheels also require a large and expensive chain-type remover. Don't fret though; you can still get home.

If a brake cable snaps, use your spare. A brake bridge cable also can be made from it. But if a derailleur cable snaps, you'll have to adjust the stops on the derailleur to a middle gear to get home.

The chain tool fixes a broken chain. Excellent directions are in the box. First, practice on some old links from a bike shop. The trick is not to push the pin all the way through the link. Turn the tool's handle until the pin is almost out, but not completely. If the chain won't separate, turn a little more, then try again.

Sticky links can cause the chain to skip when it passes through the rear derailleur. The fix is easy. Grab the chain on either side of the sticky link and twist back and forth. Use your spray lube to loosen the link. If the skipping is random, either your chain or the chainring teeth are worn. If you can pull the chain from the chainring, or if the teeth are shaped like shark's fins, it's time for a new transmission. If you've merely bent a chainring or tooth, straighten it with the Crescent wrench.

To fix a bent rear derailleur or frame hanger, insert a 6mm Allen wrench into the derailleur fixing bolt and bend it back while looking down the pulley wheels. Because index shifters require perfect frame/derailleur alignment, you might have to switch the shift lever to friction mode until you get the bike to a shop. If you break the derailleur or frame hanger, remove the cable and parts, shorten the chain, and turn the bike into a 1-speed. But don't shift the front derailleur!

If the front derailleur breaks, put the chain on the middle ring. You can still shift the rear derailleur.

A loose headset can be tightened enough to get home by using the 30mm headset wrench. But most headsets are 32 mm, so you'll have to file down the wrench.

Tighten a loose bottom bracket by hooking the blade of a flat screwdriver into a notch in the lockring. Pound the screwdriver with a rock clockwise.

Even a broken axle will sometimes work long enough to get you home, but you could permanently damage the bearing surfaces. This is also true of the headset. Sometimes walking home is worth the effort.

Equipped with the right tools and knowledge, you should return from any trip with your bike in one piece. And that means you'll be free to explore wherever you heart leads you.

◼6◼ CARE AND CLEANING

After paying all that cash for a beautiful, new, smooth-running mountain bike, you may be reluctant to head for the mud pits and dusty trails. Don't be. Although Mother Earth can make your 5-hour-old mountain bike look like it has suddenly suffered five years of deterioration, the dirt won't hurt as long as you take the necessary precautions.

What follows are some good tricks to help you keep your mountain bike working well and avoid premature parts replacement. Much of this maintenance can be done in just a few minutes.

Cleaning

The most important rule in mountain maintenance is to clean the bike frequently. Dirt acts as a grinding compound when it gets between moving parts, so the sooner you remove it, the better. In muddy or sandy conditions you may have to clean the bike after every ride.

If you're careful, you can use a car wash. Just don't let the high-pressure wand blast water into the bearings. Almost all mountain bikes have sealed bearings in the hubs and crank, but no seals are impermeable. And while we're on the subject, never ride with the crank completely submerged. The flexing from pedaling will let water through the seals. Splashing through a creek is fine; riding downstream with a snorkel isn't.

The European method of bike washing works best. You'll need a bucket of hot water, a mild detergent such as Bike Wash, three nylon-bristle brushes, a high-viscosity degreaser such as Gunk, a small screwdriver, a rinse bucket or garden hose, and an old towel. Use a floor brush for the big parts of the bike, a bottle brush for the nooks and crannies, and another bottle brush designated for greasy parts. Now move the car out of the driveway and let's get to work.

1. Initial rinse. Remove the major muck by gently spraying with the garden hose or dousing the bike with a bucketful of water. Never wipe dirt or mud from your bike with a rag—it will scratch the finish.

2. Degrease. Remove the wheels. Brush degreaser onto the derailleurs, chain, and chainrings. Mush it between the freewheel cogs. You must use a high-viscosity degreaser so it doesn't run inside sealed bearings. The thick stuff also removes surface grime from the chain without washing anything into the pins and rollers (which could cause more wear than leaving the chain dirty). Avoid aerosol degreasers—they're too light.

3. Rinse. Use water and the greasy brush to rinse the chain, derailleurs, and chainrings. A small screwdriver is handy for picking the loosened crud out of the freewheel.

4. Wheels. Start with the hub, using the clean bottle brush and a bucket of soapy water. Continue cleaning outward until you reach the rim. Scrub the rim and tire with the floor brush. Rinse.

5. Frame. Use the floor brush, then the clean bottle brush to get behind the chainrings and other hard-to-reach spots. Don't forget under the saddle. Rinse and then install the wheels.

6. Dry. Wipe off water with a towel, then put the bike in a warm place to dry thoroughly. The tubes of better mountain bikes have drain holes to allow moisture out and dry air in.

Inspection

It's easier to inspect for damage and other problems when a bike is clean. Here's the checklist.

1. Frame. Soon after you buy your mountain bike, measure its wheelbase (the distance from the rear axle to the front axle when the front wheel is straight ahead). Remeasure each time you inspect the bike. If the wheelbase grows or shrinks, something's damaged. Also look for cracks in the lugs or frame joints. These may appear as paint cracks. Inspect the tubes for bulges, dents, or ripples. If something looks suspicious, see a professional.

2. Wheels. Spin the wheels. Watch between the brake pads for dents, bulges, wobbles, and the like in the rims. Look for loose or broken spokes. Check the tires for cuts, bulges, and embedded debris. When the wheels are removed for washing, turn the axles with your fingers. Any roughness indicates the need for cone adjustment or repacking. Look for broken or bent freewheel teeth.

3. Handlebar grips. Twist them. If they move, remove them and apply rubber cement. Use enough so they slip on easily. You'll need a stickier glue such as 3M Fast Tack Trim Adhesive for soft foam grips.

4. Chain. Count 24 links and measure from the first pin to the last. A new chain should measure 12 inches. If yours is 12⅛ inches or more, replace it. Riding with a worn chain accelerates wear to chainrings and freewheel cogs. It also impairs shifting performance.

5. Derailleur alignment. This is especially critical with an index system. Sighting from behind the bike, the pulleys should be aligned vertically and parallel to the plane of the chainrings and freewheel. Anything crooked should be straightened by your dealer.

6. Brakes. Inspect the pads for wear and embedded debris. Check for frayed cables. Replace anything that is even remotely suspect. You must have reliable brakes in the outback.

7. Pedals. Occasionally remove them from the crankarms and turn the axles with your fingers, feeling for roughness or excessive play. Then look closely for fractures in the pedal body and cage. Ditto for the toe clips, if you use them. Make sure their bolts are tight.

8. Bottom bracket. With the pedals off, drape the chain around the bottom bracket shell so it doesn't touch the chainrings. Place your ear against the saddle and turn the cranks. Anything funny going on inside the bottom bracket will be amplified through the frame and become audible at the saddle. If you're not sure you like what you hear, remove the crankarms and turn the axle with your fingers to check the adjustment.

9. Headset. Grasp the top tube behind the head tube, lift the front wheel a couple of inches, and nudge the handlebar so it turns gently from side to side. If it wants to catch in the straight-ahead position, the headset is damaged. If it locks like it has auto pilot, it's ruined. The best solution for this is prevention—frequent checks to make sure the headset is properly adjusted. A loose one will clunk when you squeeze the front brake hard and rock the bike back and forth. A tight one won't let the front end pivot fully when you pick it up and nudge the handlebar. One way to get more miles from a damaged headset is to install loose ball bearings in place of the retainers. Additional bearings will fit in each race, so they won't sit in the dents that are causing the catch. You can also have the shop partially rotate the headset cups.

Lubrication

When your bike is dry, lubricate the parts you degreased and any others that may need it.

1. Chain, derailleur pulleys, rollercam brakes. The lubricant must correspond to the environment. In dry weather, use a product with a volatile carrier that penetrates well, then evaporates, leaving a viscous lubricant in place. Tri-Flow and Sta-Lube are good choices. Use a rag to protect the rear rim from overspray, and wipe away excess lubrication. Lube the exposed moving parts of a rollercam brake.

For wet weather or muddy terrain, a sticky oil works best. Try Campagnolo and Phil Wood. Although they collect dirt, they prevent anything raunchy from seeping into the chain's pins and rollers and the derailleur's pulley bushings. European cyclocross racers sometimes coat their chains with grease when the course is extra muddy. The grease simply displaces the mud.

Paraffin isn't a good choice for mountain bike chains. It doesn't last long enough, so the chain has to be removed and rewaxed too often.

2. Seatpost. If you use your mountain bike correctly, you'll frequently change your seat height. Lowering the saddle is necessary for good control on descents, so the seatpost/seat tube must be kept clean and lubricated. Remember to mark the post before you pull it from the frame in order to retain your correct saddle height. If you use a Hite-Rite seat locator, put a piece of masking tape just above the Hite-Rite sleeve. Loosen the sleeve and pull the post from the frame. Wrap a rag around a screwdriver and clean the seat tube. Lubricate the seatpost with your Campy or Phil oil and reassemble the Hite-Rite.

3. Cables. Free-sliding derailleur cables are always desirable, and they're mandatory with index shifting. Grease gets too dirty and creates drag in the system. Shimano recommends running its derailleur cables dry. If that doesn't suit you, try pure silicone spray. Braking performance can be improved by lubricating the cable end buttons at the levers.

4. Sealed bearings. Sealed bearings can and should be serviced. Carefully remove the seal with an X-Acto knife or similar tool. Be careful not to dent the seal's seat. Thorough cleaning of the internal parts is crucial, because new grease will be degraded by the old. Use a solvent such as kerosene or a degreaser and water. Wear safety goggles. Avoid getting solvent on the tires or any other rubber parts. Flush thoroughly and dry with compressed air (available by the can at photography stores). Repack the bearings with high-viscosity grease.

5. Saddle. Water and dirt can turn your saddle's supple leather covering into something akin to sandpaper. Preserve the leather by rubbing in Brooks Proofhide or Nivea skin cream. Dust the surface with baby powder or talc to make it slippery again.

6. Pump. Avoid pump failures by keeping the gasket lubed. Use petroleum jelly on leather gaskets and K-Y Jelly on rubber ones.

Finally, remember that you've got to get your mountain bike filthy in order to take care of it right. Happy (muddy and dusty) trails!

7 FEAR NOT

Your shoulders tighten like a spring. Your knuckles turn white on your handlebar grips. Your legs jerk up and down like rusty pistons. Where is the relaxed pedaling you knew just moments ago? The fear that this time you may be in over your head shoots through your body. . . .

Dealing with the fear of imminent disaster—which may or may not happen—is one of the toughest aspects of being a mountain biker. Whether you're a novice or pro, fear is part of trying to stretch out and try new techniques, new terrain, and new equipment. How can you ever hope to deal with it?

It's a complex question, because fear and anxiety are also our best safety valves. Fear is our internal signal that says "caution" or "stop!" Sometimes, fear is well grounded and should be heeded. But there are times when it should be challenged. Let's see how to recognize and successfully handle different types of fear.

Where Thrills Live

For mountain bikers, fear and anxiety come in many packages. Fear can accompany any attempt to push past your limits. Some bikers ride to their max or just beyond, seeking an adrenal rush. They drive themselves beyond comfort to a gray area where thrills live.

An experienced and competent rider from Colorado Springs expresses his feelings of fear: "I was descending the Pikes Peak trail for the first time. It was tough and really steep. There were times when I managed to get some air, and I wondered if I was gonna be able to land this thing upright. Everything was happening incredibly fast. I could just barely react in time to save myself from falling. I was riding the edge, and I was in and out of control. I loved it."

Other mountain bikers find themselves reliving their fearful experiences. Molly, from Aspen, Colorado, is an excellent rider. Her long blonde hair and freckled face give her the look of a pixie, not a mountain tyrant, but few see much of her frontside when they're riding with her. Still, she admits, "When I know I have to ride on a log over a creek, I get petrified." Asked why, she tells of several close calls when she almost fell off. But even though she didn't and thus proved her ability, she was still afraid.

Like Molly, some mountain bikers run into trouble when they recall uncomfortable experiences. The big "oh no!" shoots through their sensory system. At times like this, memories serve much like an alarm clock that rings them into a frenzied awakening. The old messages are not easily silenced.

Perhaps the most common reason for fear is the threat of injury. But letting negative feelings run wild only produces more tension, which increases the danger of damage. One bout of fear can also destroy the pleasurable experiences of a ride.

A Midwest physician and novice mountain biker expresses his discomfort: "I was riding a hilly trail in Michigan. I'd read some articles about using my front brake during descents. I was determined to use the techniques correctly. As I descended some sandy rocks, I knew I was in trouble. My wheels teetered from one slippery rock to another, and I was gaining speed. All I could think of was if I got hurt I wouldn't be able to work and I have two kids to take care of. The whole experience was very uncomfortable. I tensed, got confused, and actually came closer to an accident than I should have if I hadn't been so afraid."

It's clear that fear is not the same for all mountain bikers or all situations. What brings tension to one rider may be a welcome challenge for another. There are comfort zones and anxiety zones for each person. In addition, this can change from ride to ride depending on your attitude on the given day.

Is it just a quirk, or do you have control over whether your potentially dangerous cycling experiences are wonderful or fearful? There's no question that if you learn to deal with fear, you have more control over the quality and enjoyment of your mountain biking. Whether your fear stems from pushing your limits, recalling an uncomfortable experience, or concerns about injuries—or something else—here are three basic techniques that will help you defuse high-anxiety situations.

Focus on the Moment

You can handle many difficult situations by focusing on what you need to do right now.

If you want to become a better mountain biker, you must expose yourself to new techniques and untried terrain. But doing so can be unpleasant if you feel you can't handle what's happening. When you sense that things are happening to you, you are out of control. You feel helpless. Your confidence disappears and your skills deteriorate. You imagine all sorts of disastrous things might happen, and they become bigger than life. The chance of an accident increases. The sad truth is, you're pulling your own strings.

So pull them in a positive way. Take charge of your tough situation by focusing on what you need to do at the moment. Don't tune into fear and anxiety, or they'll become the center of your attention instead of what it takes to pull you through.

To solve this dilemma, tell yourself what you need to do now. Say, "I need to slow my thoughts and the speed of my bike. That's right, brake with even pressure. And now I need to ride to the left of that boulder. . . ." Giving yourself directions that focus on the present and immediate future provide all the input you can handle in a tense situation. Ride the terrain under your wheels, and you'll perform better and more safely.

Give Yourself Positive Instructions

When some riders try to take charge of a tough situation, they tell themselves what not to do. As children, one of the first words we learned was "no!" So it's no surprise that today we spend an inordinate amount of time telling ourselves what to avoid doing. But negative statements often hurt confidence and provide incomplete, impractical messages. The truth is that in order to improve, you need to understand what you need to do, not what you shouldn't do.

So give yourself positive instructions, and treat yourself like your own best friend. Be encouraging, because when you say to yourself, "Don't hit that rock," your mind actually fixates on the rock. Not hitting it could mean going to the left or to the right or stopping short. These options may confuse you, and your body will reflect this mental chaos. Conversely, if you say to yourself, "Steer to the left of that rock," your mind is telling your body exactly what to do. Little or no interpretation is necessary. Your instructions are crystal clear, so you're much more likely to be successful.

Nurture a "Can Do" Attitude

This takes self-awareness and self-examination. It also requires courage and the willingness to look at your negative statements. When you feel your wheels sliding or your speed increasing too rapidly, the ideal response is to automatically switch into a positive outlook, feeling that you're capable of handling the situation.

To develop a can do attitude, examine your strengths and weaknesses as a rider. This will help you understand your limitations and the areas in which you're willing to "stretch" your ability. Consider your recent rides. What have you done well? Concentrate on things you want to improve, not how many mistakes you've made. Then you can map the exploration of new experiences.

Growth has a price. When learning new riding techniques, you're bound to encounter situations that make you uncomfortable. It's through experiencing and overcoming such anxious discomfort that you'll expand your skills and horizons.

Meeting the Challenge

When confronted with a new challenge, slow down. Look at what's happening. If the situation is so far beyond your current talents that you feel you're getting in over your head, stop. If the situation is in the "uncomfortable but doable" category, be positive. Accept it as a learning experience. Sure it's a little frightening but it's also exciting. Encourage yourself, and you can make it.

A can do attitude requires giving yourself the freedom to make errors and recover. After all, even if you don't ride perfectly, you are learning. Momentary anxieties and disappointments are inevitable. One difference between an accomplished mountain biker and one who doesn't progress is the ability to bounce back with renewed effort. Self-statements such as "Oops, I still need to work on the maneuver" rather than "Boy, I need to get my act together and stop being so afraid, or I'll never get this" have great impact on the way you see yourself and the extent to which you'll ride well.

Many fine riders practice their anxious moments when they're not riding. They mentally replay tough situations and positive solutions. Then when tough situations actually occur, they react instinctively and confidently.

Mountain biking isn't meant to be a walk in the park. It's

demanding and sometimes risky. While excessive fear can inhibit our progress, a healthy respect for danger can protect us by keeping us within sane boundaries. Therefore, it's not smart to challenge all fear, just that which doesn't result from a sound cause.

Always remember that your fear is exactly that—your fear. Only you can decide when to heed it and when to battle it. Only you can determine how much and how fast you want to push. Watch and listen to others, but obey your own guidelines and you'll meet the challenges meaningful to you.

Part Two

RIDING
TECHNIQUES

8 EIGHT SKILL BUILDERS

There's a rumor going around that 80 percent of the people who own mountain bikes never ride them off-road. Perhaps you harbor Walter Mitty dreams of scaling peaks and descending on ethereal knobby wings, but you're uncertain of your skills. Indeed, the biggest obstacle preventing great road riders from becoming great off-road riders is skill. Not that it takes more or less skill to ride on- or off-road. The off-road environment simply requires a different bag of tricks than the highway. So we've compiled eight ways for you to quickly acquire the skills that will take you from road warrior to mud pup.

Ride lots. This is what former professional road racer Eddy Merckx replied when asked how to become a world-class cyclist. What he meant was to ride often over great distances. For our purposes, this translates into riding a lot through parking lots and fields. Use your mountain bike for everything. Ride it to the store. Ride it in traffic. Cut across parking lots and learn how to hop over curbs without denting your rims. Take shortcuts across fields and construction sites. Spend a few minutes fooling around on dirt piles or taking a few laps around the impromptu BMX tracks that inevitably sprout there. Become familiar with your mountain bike's fit and handling characteristics before venturing into the outback.

Discover observed trials. Riding over obstacles is actually a competitive sport called "observed trials." The object of the game is to negotiate an obstacle course or "section" without falling or putting your foot down. There are usually several sections of varying difficulty for a given trials event. If you're not daring enough to enter a trials event, you should at least watch one. You'll be amazed at the feats a skilled rider can perform.

To find a local trials event, check the bulletin board at a shop that sells mountain bikes or contact the National Off-Road Bicycle Association (NORBA), 1750 E. Boulder St., #4, Colorado Springs, CO 80909.

Toe the line. Once you're a skilled backyard technician, it's time to venture into the real off-road environment. "The line" is off-roader jargon for the best possible path—be it uphill, downhill, through mud, or over rocks. With practice, the best line through the wild becomes as obvious to an off-road rider as the painted white line is to a road rider. Find a loop or out-and-back trail that's 1 mile long or less. Ideally, it should have a variety of riding surfaces and terrain, including challenging hills and descents. It should be tough enough so that initially you can't ride parts of it.

Ride the trail often and experiment with different techniques for surmounting the natural obstacles. For example, if you get bogged down in mud when riding around a puddle, try pedaling through it. Ground that's too firm to allow seepage is sometimes firm enough to ride over. Try the left side, the middle, and the right side of each trail section. Sometimes the worst looking route is the most rideable. Sometimes not.

Try riding the trail at different speeds in a variety of gears. Sometimes it pays to pick your way along, while other trouble spots are best negotiated swiftly. In time, you'll be able to identify a good line through unknown territory and know just what it takes to ride it smoothly.

Ride with others. To reinforce what you learn on your trail, cycle with better riders at least once a week. Following their line is a great way to learn off-road rhythm. Just shift where they shift, stand where they stand, and ride where they ride. Hanging out with good riders will also give you the inside line on what equipment works best. They can help you choose tires that are best suited for your part of the country. Plus, they'll probably have opinions on which shoes, toe clips, brake pads, and other options work best.

Master the uphills. This technique is a graduate-level balancing act. Besides steadying your bike side to side, you must balance your weight fore and aft in order to keep your rear wheel from spinning and your front wheel on the ground. Some riders do this by sitting on the saddle and adjusting their fore/aft weight distribution by bending at the waist. Others stand and lean closer to or farther from the bar. Get one of your newfound off-road buddies to ride your practice trail with you. Watch what he or she does to negotiate the hills. Mimic the technique. You may surprise yourself.

Relax on descents. "How can I possibly relax on an off-road descent?" you may wonder. The answer sounds like a Zen riddle. You can't go fast if you don't relax—and you must start slowly. If your arms and legs are stiff when you're descending, you'll become airborne or get knocked sideways by every bump and pebble. Relaxed arms and legs act as shock absorbers that keep your tires in contact with the ground at high speed, like a downhill skier who compresses his body to "absorb" bumps and ruts.

If you're inexperienced, it's best to start slowly. Find a moderate downhill about 200 yards long—it could even be part of your practice trail. Drop your saddle about 3 inches, hold the handlebar grips firmly (but without whitening your knuckles), place your index and middle fingers on the brake levers, level the crankarms, stand, and roll slowly down the hill. Check your speed by gently pumping the brakes.

These slow-motion rehearsals will accustom you to the basic downhiller's position, which you can modify as the pitch of the land and your speed changes. Generally, the steeper the grade, the farther back you should shift your weight. This will keep you from pitching over the handlebar and prevent the rear wheel from losing traction.

When you've mastered one hill, try the same technique on gradually steeper inclines until you're comfortable on anything you encounter.

Go to school. If you feel you need a more structured environment for learning off-road skills, consider going to school. One we know of is the Mountain Bike School and Touring Center at Mount Snow, West Dover, Vermont. It offers multiple-day seminars that cover all the basics, plus general outdoor necessities such as map and compass use. You don't even need to bring a bike—they have them, too. For more information, call 1-800-451-4211.

Lately other downhill ski areas have begun offering mountain bike instruction and rentals in the summer. Check your local alpine resort to see if they have such a program.

Move to Marin County, California. Or pick any other mountain biking epicenter. There must be something funny in the water. Certain places seem to have an excess of great mountain bikers. Ask anyone in Crested Butte, Colorado, or Marin—they'll tell you how great they are. And if a trendy ZIP code doesn't make you a great off-roader, you can always fall back on the other tips.

9 USING YOUR EYES

There's a line on the slickrock in Utah's canyon country, a fairly easy line, maybe a 4 on a scale of 10. You drop into a small depression, then power up a short climb to curve around a shoulder of red rock. Cleaning it should be a snap except for one thing—an adjacent 300-foot-deep chasm. Fall to the right and you die.

Yet if this line is approached with your focus firmly fixed in the present and on where you want to go, riding it is no problem. The abyss may be in your peripheral vision, but your eyes must watch only the path. In fact, the key to cleaning any technical section is the same: Where your eyes lead, your bike follows. Still, few dare try this line; the cliff acts as a magnet that pulls on the brain.

There's nothing new about using your eyes to lead your body. "Keep your eye on the ball" is practically the mantra of American athletics. But the reverse—trying not to stare at what you want to avoid—often seems impossible. Our eyes lock onto a nasty rock in the path as if we could visually fend it off. We can't. Instead, the front wheel bangs into it. Even if we manage to steer clear, we're still doomed, because our sense of balance is nullified by our gaze. Our passage deteriorates into jerky movements and awkward recovery as we teeter on the verge of a crash.

To avoid these problems, learn a new way to see. Instead

of staring at the trail with "hard eyes," try to lightly scan it. Focus on specific points just long enough to register their location. Keep your eyes sweeping over the terrain and be aware of your peripheral vision; that's where the optimum line will appear. How far ahead to scan depends on your speed. In technical sections it's often wise to scan no farther than the length of your bike, while during a screaming descent you might want to search 100 feet ahead.

Look for the path of least resistance, the easiest to ride. Think of the rocks, logs, and stumps as markers that define your line rather than as obstacles to avoid. Not staring at them seems difficult, but once you accept that your line is found between them, it becomes easy.

Our preoccupation with rocks and stumps is understandable. After all, they can make us crash, and we might get hurt. It's all very logical, except for one thing: The fear of crashing becomes a self-fulfilling prophecy. Muscles tense, we worry about what lies ahead, and our thoughts leave the present. The line is blown, and our confidence is shattered.

Yet another result of staring at obstacles is forgetting to breathe. We take a big breath as if we're diving into water, then hold it while we attempt to force the front wheel through a minefield of rocks. None of this is conscious, and that's precisely the problem: We're not paying attention. Trail riding demands total awareness of our actions and the terrain we're passing over.

Breathing to a mountain biker is like foot tapping to a musician; it sets the rhythm. Slow, relaxed breathing calms us, while hard, strong breaths can urge us to make greater efforts. By consciously maintaining a steady breathing rhythm, we ensure a strong flow of oxygen to our muscles. More important, conscious breathing helps keep our attention fixed in the present and all our energy focused on riding.

10 BIKING THE LINE

Every trail, every hill has an optimum line. Pick the right one and cruise; pick the wrong one and flounder. The challenge for mountain bikers, as well as for surfers, board sailors, climbers, skiers, river runners, and philosophers, is to recognize and follow this line. Our ride then turns into a symphony of motion, a blending of the land's rhythms and ours. We jam. Previously unsolvable problems slip past like silk over steel. We're dialed in and riding faster and smoother than ever.

Following these lines isn't luck or magic, it's skill. Learning it depends on the rider's attitude and willingness to concentrate and practice.

The first step is honing the basics, becoming so comfortable on the bike that riding is second nature—shifting gears until you can hit the right cog at any time; being able to anticipate your braking. In football parlance it's termed "getting your reps," so that the moves come without thinking.

Your goal is instinctive action guided by accumulated wisdom. Practice riding as slowly as possible through gnarly terrain, and practice rushing through. Momentum can compensate for weak riding skills and is sometimes the only thing that will get you through tough sections. Practice slow-motion riding until you can "track stand" for a few seconds at a time.

The objective is to clear your head of debris and keep the gray matter from becoming cluttered with questions and doubts. Fast, technical singletracking requires instant response and total commitment. Shut off the mental chatter. Tune into the land, and the lines will leap out.

The slickrock of southeastern Utah provides the finest test of the art of line finding. In theory, rock riders can follow any line they want. In reality, cleanable lines on this vast, rolling, ancient seabed are camouflaged to look like the rest of the rock, and finding them takes concentration and sensitivity.

Often, the difference between lines that let you ride and those that don't is a matter of inches or degrees. To ride cleanly, you have to ignore the magnificent view and focus on the subtle shifts in the rock's surface. A 200-foot face of curving sandstone that looks rideable from all directions may turn out to have one or two lines with a margin of error narrower than half the width of the handlebar.

If your angle of attack slips and you scrape a pedal, you're out of the action. If you turn left a foot too late, you can't get the front end around. The front wheel drifts, and suddenly the tires no longer hold. A bit of lichen, a patch of loose sand, or even a tiny unnoticed step in the rock surface defeats you.

It's not how much power you can apply to the cranks, it's how you apply it. Despite what appears as unlimited traction, power must be moderately and precisely applied. Riders with reputations as "hammers" are often chagrined to find themselves afoot, while weaker-legged riders disappear over the top of yet another rock face. The difference is finesse—studying the terrain and going with it rather than fighting it. On rock this means watching for shifts in surface contours and conditions. On steep faces it means looking for slight ramps angling up and across that might make for superior purchase. If a straight-line attack looks feasible, pick a line where lichen is minimal—it'll have better traction and won't harm the lichen, a fragile part of the desert's fabric of life. Apply just enough power to keep going. And apply it smoothly, especially when riding out of the saddle. *Keep an eye on where you want the front wheel to go, not where you don't want it to go.*

Because you can descend steeper routes than you can climb, picking precise descent routes isn't as critical. It's important, however, to moderate your use of the rear brake. A skidding tire won't slow you down as much as a nonskidding one, and it leaves a black streak on the rock. The front brake is your source of stopping power. Pick the smoothest line possible and avoid dropping the front wheel into sharp depressions or sand traps while braking hard.

The advantage of learning all this on slickrock is the total freedom of choice it provides. On roads and trails choices are limited; we have to go where they lead. On rock the selection is infinite, with a spectrum of gradations to choose from. You can turn up the intensity at any time by taking a steeper line. Rock riding expands our perceptions of what's possible.

The last part of the quest for the ultimate line is knowing where you are, where you've been, and what effect your passage will have. Think of your track as a delicate pen stroke in a Japanese painting, or imagine your track spinning out behind the bike, a visual record of your passage. You flow over the contours, carving graceful curves, following the path of least resistance, leaving minimal traces.

Each of us has a dark side. We're tempted to take short-cuts, arrogantly crushing vegetation. A second of convenience wipes out years of growth. A brush stroke turns into the slash of a saber.

We have to balance our desire to push our limits with the impact that pushing them has, otherwise the paintings we create will be flawed. Like the insulated and isolated motor-heads who hear only their screaming engines, who smell only their own exhaust, and who feel only a machine's power as they gouge paths straight up hills, we'd be aliens from a strange world.

11 GOING UP?

The early Marin County bikers had climbing wired: Just throw the bikes in the back of a truck. This was your basic, no-sweat, maximum-grins vision of life. Then the American work ethic reared its head and the free fun tickets were spurned. To ride down, you had to ride up, and the sport was dramatically changed. Going up required stiff frames, light weight, and multiple gears. Laid-back angles and long wheelbases were replaced by steep angles and short wheelbases. Yet despite the improvements, climbing remains mountain biking's universal bugaboo.

It needn't be. Climbing isn't as difficult as most people think. We make it hard by attempting hills we're not prepared to climb. Conversely, we also have the means to make climbing easy.

First, check your gearing. If it's what your bike came with, it's probably too high. Switch your 26- or 28-tooth granny chainring for a 24-inch. Make sure your freewheel's biggest cog has at least 30 teeth. If you're young and strong with perfect knees, go with 28. If you're just getting into the sport and aren't especially fit, choose 32 or 34. You may feel foolish barely moving while spinning away like a berserk squirrel in a runaway cage, but you'll learn to love it.

If your tires aren't 2.125-inch knobbies, get some. Ride with about 40 pounds of pressure or less in places where traction is minimal. Improvements in traction will be dramatic compared with tires that are narrower and pumped to higher pressure. Instead of bouncing off rocks, your tires will roll over them. The extent to which performance is affected by tire pressure is probably far greater than you imagine.

Shorten your handlebar and lower the stem. The bar should be about the width of your shoulders (21 to 24 inches). Slide the shifters, brake levers, and grips inward on your existing bar to find the length that suits you, then cut off the excess. Sink the stem into the steerer tube until the handlebar is an inch or two lower than the saddle. Try different heights until you find what's efficient for you. The more extreme the climbing, the lower you'll want the bar, but the final position is always a compromise between the requirements of ascending and descending. The stem's extension also impacts on climbing efficiency, but this gets into the complexities of bike fit, an article in itself.

Contrary to popular opinion, 17-inch or shorter chainstays are not necessary for maximum traction. Bikes with 19-inch chainstays could climb like goats if their wheelbases were correctly proportioned. The key is the front/center dimension (the distance from the center of the front wheel to the center of the bottom bracket). Rear wheel traction requires only enough weight to keep the tire from slipping, and no more. The remaining weight has to be on the front wheel for precise steering.

A rider's center of mass is located just above the waist and midway through the body. Imagine an arrowlike pendulum suspended from this point. If you're standing in perfect balance on a flat floor, the arrow will point to a spot between your feet and roughly midway from toe to heel. Call this spot the balance point. On a bike, it's directly in line with the wheels' contact points and somewhere between them. The distance between that balance point and each wheel's contact point determines how much weight each wheel carries. Move the balance point forward, and the percentage of weight borne by the front wheel is increased, while the rear wheel's is decreased. Move it backward and the reverse is true.

If the plane upon which the bike and rider rolls tilts upward, the arrow will swing backward. Continue this tilting

Photograph 2-1. The key to successful climbing is to shift your body forward, keeping weight on the front wheel.

and eventually the balance point will coincide with the rear wheel's contact point, and all weight will press on it. Tilt the plane steeper yet and the balance point will move behind the tire's contact point, causing the bike and rider to pitch over backward. The same rearward movement of the balance point can also be caused by the rider sliding back on the saddle. If the rider moves back far enough, bike and rider will pitch over. Therefore, the problem on climbs is keeping weight on the front wheel, not on the rear. (The reverse is true on downhills.)

Importance of Weight Shift

Basically, when people fail to climb a hill it is because they're not strong enough to keep spinning the cranks or because they can't maintain the correct line. The former is cured by lower gearing and more strength, the latter through practice and shifting forward on the saddle.

Forward weight shift is the key to becoming a first-rate climber. By moving toward the nose of the saddle (on shallow slopes, a slight forward lean is sufficient), your balance point is moved forward, offsetting its rearward movement caused by the hill's slope. The objective is to remain balanced between the wheels. This doesn't mean the wheels are equally weighted, just that there's enough weight on the rear to maintain traction. If you shift forward slightly, the rear wheel will lose traction; if you shift back a bit, the front end will waver. You're perfectly balanced when weight can be shifted fore and aft with only a subtle movement. So solid is the position that you can stand without affecting your balance point.

This balancing is dynamic, not static. The bike has to be free to move with the terrain while your torso remains quietly suspended over it. The suspension system linking torso and bike is your arms and legs. To function effectively, they have to be flexible and strong, especially the arms. After severe climbs, arms are usually as tired as legs.

On radically steep slopes, pivot your wrists downward and keep your elbows low and in. Imagine a plane parallel to the hubs extending back from the hand grips. If your elbows are slightly below this plane, the resulting force will be back and down with a fraction pressing the front wheel to the ground. If your elbows are slightly above this plane, your pull will be back and up with a fraction lifting the front wheel.

The last ingredient for climbing is moderation. Low gears aren't for power but to moderate your power. Low gearing equals high torque, and high torque means the rear tire can easily be spun on loose surfaces. Therefore, the objective is to apply just enough torque to maintain forward motion without losing traction. Like trying to run on ice, it has to be done carefully, smoothly, and slowly. But the problem when riding so slowly is to keep the bike upright, which brings us full circle to shifting weight forward to maintain steering control.

Now you see why climbing is a question of balance, not power or traction. Stay balanced over your bike, ride with low gears and fat, soft tires, and keep cranking no matter what. Soon you'll be flattening the steepest slopes with impressive regularity.

12 STARTING ON A HILL

The chunk of wet deadfall you failed to notice shoots out from under your rear tire like a slippery watermelon seed. Your forward motion comes to an abrupt, crank-spinning halt. You flop forward, almost smacking your chest on the handlebar. Your right foot flies off the pedal and stabs uselessly in the air as the bike starts tipping over. All that saves you is a quick leg brace and a hard squeeze of the brakes. You're at a dead stop in the middle of a dishearteningly long, steep hill.

Three choices confront you. You can push or portage the bike to the top, you can go down and try it again, or you can continue the climb from where you are.

The first choice is probably the most popular. The second is the least, because few riders care to repeat work already accomplished. The third is the most tempting but also the most difficult. It means remounting on the same terrain that just stopped you. Restarting never fails to be harder than riding all the way up on the first attempt.

As you stand there, you realize it should be possible to

pedal to the top. The trail is a mix of bedrock, packed dirt, and loose gravel. Traction is thin and the slope steep, so to get going again you need an instant burst of power for forward momentum, but you also must keep a straight line; if you "saw" the handlebar you'll never get moving. There's also the little matter of an upside-down toe clip. How the heck can you get your foot into it?

That last problem is the easiest to solve: you don't, or at least not right away. Put one foot into a clip and forget about the other. Use the back of that pedal and consider yourself lucky if you make it to the top without having to bail out again (which is a lot easier to do if one foot is already free).

Getting started requires delicate balance. Lowering your saddle can help, especially when you're new to this game. Make sure you're in the lowest gear. Now check the trail. Look for a slight leveling of the slope, or a flat spot behind a rock or log, or even a shallow depression. This is where you want to place your rear tire. Make sure the front isn't behind a stone or other obstacle. If there's a rock, a low embankment, or anything else you can stand on, so much the better. Get on it and throw a leg over the bike. Put your foot into the toe clip and backpedal to the start of your power stroke. You need to apply a smooth, even force to get the maximum forward movement.

Now decide whether to stand or sit during the first stroke. You'll probably be able to sit only if you've lowered the saddle or are standing on something.

Sitting improves traction because your weight is over the rear wheel. But it can also cause you to immediately pop a wheelie or veer to the side. Standing lets you maintain pressure on the front wheel while simultaneously applying maximum power. But with insufficient weight on the rear wheel, there's also the likelihood of your first crank stroke causing another abrupt spin-out.

An alternative exists, and here's an example of how it works. Stand over the top tube, right foot at the start of the power stroke, left foot lightly on the ground, torso comfortably bent forward, hands squeezing the brake levers. Sit on the tip of the saddle so you are pressing back rather than down.

As you release the brakes, simultaneously rock the bike forward and push off with the left foot, putting your weight on the right pedal. Now here's the tricky part: Apply power to the crank with great restraint. Don't spin the rear wheel. Use your arms to pull gently down and back; if you pull up on the bar you'll wheelie. Press back on the saddle in response to the rear wheel's needs. You've got to have a high degree of sensitivity to the tire's traction.

Focus on a spot ahead of the line you want to take. Imagine your eyes pulling you to it. If traction is good, shift slightly forward so you're crouched over the top tube and either just off or barely touching the saddle. At such a slow speed it's important to keep pressure on the front wheel so you can steer accurately. The more technical the terrain or the more constricted your path, the more important this is. Balance your pedal thrusts to minimize lateral movement of the bike. Concentrate on smoothness.

If traction is poor, put more weight on the saddle while pulling strongly down on the handlebar. The trick is to keep pressure on the front wheel while putting as much weight as possible on the rear wheel.

A tree or bush can also help you get started. Position your bike close to it and hold on with one hand. Put both feet into the clips. If it's a bush, you won't actually be able to push off, but you can with a tree. These starts are best done when seated, so be prepared to smoothly slide forward during your first or second pedal stroke. You need to get far enough forward on the saddle to center your weight. Then you can make weight shifts with minimal movement.

Okay, you've started successfully and have made two or three pedal strokes. But now your front wheel is about to hit a slight step in the path. You don't yet have enough momentum to carry you over, so you must quickly create it.

Time the beginning of your next power stroke so it coincides with the tire meeting the obstacle. This might require a slight pause or even a quick backpedal. Now apply the power and lower your torso while simultaneously raising the front end of the bike. If you're a skier, you'll recognize the term down-unweighting, which is what this movement is. You can unweight whatever is supporting your body by either jumping up or by dropping down. Both create a fractional moment when no weight presses down. What makes this movement a challenge is the need to unweight only the front wheel and avoid popping a wheelie. You want to skim the wheel over the step while keeping the rear wheel weighted for traction.

Down-unweighting accomplishes the same thing as up-unweighting, or jumping the front wheel up. Both result in unweighting, which naturally leads to weighting. It's like landing on the floor after a jump, legs bent, muscles flexed. Think of it as the equivalent of compressing a spring. For a second, tires are compressed into maximum contact with the ground. Your muscles are tensed, lungs empty. Everything is set for an explosive upward and forward thrust. In short, you've just created the momentum necessary to get the rear wheel up and over the step.

Your torso is low, arms bent. Just before the rear tire hits the step, release your stored energy by surging forward with your body. As you cross the step, immediately pull the bike up behind you. All this must be done subtly and quickly or you'll lose traction. The moment the rear tire clears the step, put your weight back for traction and reapply power to the pedals.

If you've succeeded, you'll be totally "jacked." The hill is yours. Hold your elbows in and down, balance on the saddle tip, shift weight with each pedal stroke, and you'll find yourself gaining strength. By the time you hit the summit, you'll be flying. That fragile start zone has been convincingly left behind, and now you're back in the fray.

13 MAXIMUM TRACTION

The most obvious difference between good and mediocre mountain bikers is the ability to get traction. You can have the legs of Andy Hampsten and the lungs of Greg LeMond, but you won't do well off-road unless you can consistently transfer all the power to the ground.

Getting traction (or "hooking up") on off-road terrain requires unique skills. For road riders, traction is almost never a problem. On a mountain bike, though, it's a big issue. Lack of it will keep you from scaling a steep hill, riding through a sandy wash, or moving ahead at all in snow or mud. But just what is traction?

For our purposes, traction can be defined as the transmission of force from the tire to the riding surface, via friction. This force can result from accelerating, braking, or cornering. The amount of force that can be transferred horizontally depends largely on the vertical force on the tire. If you have all your body weight over one wheel, for instance, the other wheel won't grip. We'll be focusing on accelerating rather than stopping or cornering, but the principles are the same. Here then are the four fundamentals of good traction.

Prepare your equipment. Generally, relatively inexperienced off-road riders either don't know what tire pressure they're using, or their tires are inflated to the maximum recommended pressure. This is fine for cruising on hard-packed surfaces where traction isn't a concern, but the instant the going gets rough, these folks have trouble going.

Typically, novice riders blame themselves rather than realizing they could improve their performance with only a few minor equipment modifications. For one, learn to adjust your tire pressure in accordance with your weight, riding style, and surface conditions. For instance, if you're riding a slick forest trail where the traction demands are severe (steep climbs, tight corners, mud), maintain low tire pressure. In most cases, tire pressure should range between 20 and 40 psi. It's a continual compromise between the need for adequate traction and low rolling resistance.

If you don't own a mountain bike but are planning to buy one, take a tape measure with you to the shop. As far as traction is concerned, the most important element of a bike's design is the distance from the center of the crank axle to the center of the slot in the rear dropout. This is called chainstay length. The shorter this measurement, the better your grip can be. Since this isn't an adjustable parameter, buy the bike with the shortest stays you feel comfortable with. The definition of short depends on your height and build (a taller rider can get away with longer stays), but, generally, if you're shorter than 6 feet, look for chainstays of 17.25 inches or less.

Stand up. When the trail turns nasty, don't be afraid to get your rear end off the saddle. Standing enables you to use the strength in your upper body to dynamically pulse the rear tire. This is done by bending your elbows, lowering your head toward the stem, and pulling back and up on the handlebar at the beginning of each pedal stroke. Don't let your rear end come forward, though. Such a technique also enables you to keep more of your weight over the front wheel, which facilitates steering. Stand up only when you have to, though, as this method takes a great deal of energy.

Read the surface. Jean-Claude Killy, the former downhill ski champion, once claimed that in a race down a gentle beginner's slope with no ski poles, he could beat anyone. This stemmed from his ability to quickly read surfaces—to choose a path at a single glance that offered the most advantageous slope and the fastest snow. A good mountain biker does the same thing, whether traveling uphill, downhill, or on the flats.

When riding on a fire trail or jeep road, occasionally glance farther ahead than normal. Look for loose gravel, ruts, rock slabs, and hard-packed clay sideslopes. Be aware of changes in ground color, too. For instance, in dry climates darker soil usually harbors more moisture and better traction. Learn to bypass soft, loose areas by riding up onto hard clay banks or rock slabs. If you can't avoid a soft area, look for undisturbed soil or places with grassy reinforcement. Try to plot a course that won't require abrupt changes in direction, since turning wastes traction that could otherwise be used for forward drive.

Maintain your speed. This is simple. When approaching a section of trail that looks as if it's inhabited by the Prince of Antitraction, shift to the proper gear *ahead of time,* and hit the section with as much inertia as is reasonable and controllable. You wouldn't approach a difficult climb slowly unless you were really strong or wanted to show off, and the same goes for a soft patch of deep sand or snow. Be aggressive and anticipate the situation. Then, once you're in the bad stuff, accelerate some more, keeping your front wheel light to reduce the chance of digging in and flipping.

A good mountain biker must think about traction all the time. With these four principles in mind, you should be able to ride more places and have lots more fun. Just remember that it takes practice.

14 DOWNSHIFTING

Downshifting in the dirt requires anticipation. The problem is that off-road deceleration is fast, far more so than on pavement. So while roadies smoothly click their way through the gears one cog at a time while maintaining a constant cadence, mountain bikers downshift three gears in one jump, even with their wide ratios. And that can mean a loss of momentum unless you know what to do.

Smooth shifts result from gear changes under minimal load. If you're standing while climbing a hill and can barely force the cranks around, your transmission is under maximum load. Attempting a shift can damage it. Nonetheless, that's precisely what novice mountain bikers do. The latest derailleurs are marvels of efficiency and can often handle forced shifts, but their life will be shortened.

The trick is to shift before you have to. If you see a hill ahead that will require downshifting, do so beforehand, even if that means coasting into the hill. Don't worry about losing momentum; you'll lose it fast enough anyway. And don't worry about shifting into too low a gear; it's better to err by going low than high. Upshifting is always easier than downshifting.

When you're in too high a gear on a steep hill and either have to downshift or walk, you can still pull off a smooth, quiet shift. What you need is an acceleration burst with a brief power letup and simultaneous gear shift. Stand and jam a few strokes. Then sit down, relax the pressure, and shift gears, all at the same time. The bike will slow down until the shift is complete, but you'll quickly regain any lost speed. The burst of acceleration, though, has to be strong enough so you can coast for a moment. That might be for only one pedal stroke, but that's enough to relax the strain on the chain so it can drop smoothly onto the lower gear.

The front derailleur downshift is the hardest under load. Component companies have gone to great lengths to design capable equipment, but even their best front derailleurs sometimes refuse to downshift. With a modicum of anticipation, though, any front derailleur can be reliable. Just lighten the chain pressure by pedaling softly, and the chain will thunk right over.

While there's no absolute rule on how and when to shift, certain guidelines have proved reliable. If you're heading down a short hill and see a climb coming, coast down in the gear you'll need for the climb. If you're in a hurry, jam on down in your highest gear, but just before you hit the hill, accelerate, then throw the chain to the appropriate climbing gear. You may lose speed, but you'll more than make up for it in climbing efficiency, because no time will be wasted shifting under load.

On long, sustained climbs, use a lower gear than you'd need for a short hill. Ration your energy so you get to the top with enough to continue. Spinning in a low gear is more efficient than pushing a big gear, which can wear you out long before you get to the top. And if you hit an unexpected steep spot while using a high gear, you may wind up on foot because the transmission refuses to downshift with so much strain on the chain. Even if you bring it off, you might be so tired that the new gear is also a struggle, and you'll arrive on top thoroughly whipped.

On technical downhills, shift to the middle chainring and the largest cog to reduce chain-slap on the stay. Don't shift to too low a gear for technical passages that are relatively flat, because some pedal resistance is necessary for maneuvering; instead, shift gears before the passage. On descents, downshift to whatever gear will match your slowest anticipated speed. When you have to slow down abruptly to negotiate some technical problem, you can concentrate on braking and picking your line, since you're already in the appropriate gear. The novice invariably upshifts for the downhill, then attempts to thread through a rocky section in a gear much too high. True, you can shift and brake simultaneously, but doing so separately is much easier.

The key is riding with your eyes and mind. Scan the path ahead, anticipate gearing needs, and shift while pedaling softly. Soon, changing gears will become a cohesive part of the whole, done instinctively rather than reactively. Your passage will be fluid as you flow over obstacles with eyes, hands, and feet moving in concert, like those of a hot pianist in a groove.

15 GIVING YOUR BIKE A RIDE

Bank on it—sometime, somewhere, somehow you're going to push, pull, or pack your bike up a hill. The rider who actually enjoys it, though, is rare. Some riders even resent it.

They shouldn't. Along with fat tires and flat handlebars, the shoulder strap is what clearly defines a mountain bike.

In the first place, no one's forcing you to attempt hills you can't clean. If you always want to ride to the top, just tackle hills where you can. But be sure your gearing is low enough. Too high a granny gear forces more riders afoot than any other factor.

If you're adventurous at all, though, you'll be on foot sometimes no matter how low your gearing. Ironically, the higher your skill level, the greater the likelihood you'll walk, since you'll forever be seeking harder challenges. Exploring is still fun, even when that means hauling your bike to reach some great singletrack.

The key to bike packing is attitude. Don't push your bike up a hill like a laundry cart; stand up and carry it on your shoulder. You haven't been defeated, you've pushed the limits. Getting to that point required riding over terrain where the average person wouldn't walk. You gave it your best shot. Know it.

For comfort, a shoulder strap makes a big difference; you can walk upright and enjoy where you are. If on singletrack, you'll present a narrow profile and won't be forced off the trail. Don't forget to change shoulders once in awhile, but do forget about the crud on the chain; little will get on your clothes.

To lift your bike without strain, stand next to it and reach across with your opposite hand, palm down and thumb back. Grab the top tube balance point. Lift the bike onto your near shoulder while reaching through the main triangle with your other arm and grabbing the handlebar stem to steady it.

If the section you need to walk is short, you're better off pushing the bike, otherwise inertia might take over and soon you'll be walking up hills you could have cleaned. Pushers tend to remount earlier than carriers.

When pushing, flip the bike up onto its back wheel while holding the handlebar. Now you can roll it in front of you without having to leave a narrow trail. This technique is especially efficient in brush where branches are forever snagging pedals, derailleurs, and levers.

Consider lugging your bike up a hill an opportunity to reciprocate. After all, look what it's done for you!

16 BIKING WHILE LOADED

Riding a loaded mountain bike is a challenge. Handling is sluggish, and hills you normally breeze over can turn into demons of difficulty. But if you plan to go on multiday backcountry excursions, you'll probably have to carry a load. Of course, you can keep the weight down if you're willing to give up the comforts of home.

You can carry your gear on the bike or on your back. Racks and panniers are the choice for graded dirt roads and improved jeep trails, but for singletracking, bushwhacking, and crossing passes where portaging is required, a backpack is the ticket. You'll never see a road rider with a backpack, but paved roads don't demand the kind of bike handling required in the backcountry.

A load will slow the bike's response, but you can minimize the effect by using front and rear panniers to optimize weight distribution. Theories about distributing weight on road bikes don't always apply to mountain biking, where speeds are slower and handling is more demanding. However, there is a simple, logical approach.

You'll need two bathroom scales and someone to help. Place the scales next to a wall and put a wheel on each. On your unladen bike, assume your normal riding position, maintaining balance by bracing an elbow against the wall. The scale readings allow you to calculate the percentage of total weight on each wheel.

Now, pack your gear, take another reading, and adjust the load to reflect the unladen proportions. Achieving the perfect distribution may interfere with access to some items, but because you'll spend more time riding than digging through panniers, give handling your priority. Fine-tune your setup by shifting weight between front and rear until the handling feels right. Once you've established the correct proportions, make a note.

Because you've added considerable mass, particularly to the front end, handling will feel different. Front wheel response will be diminished, and steering will seem sluggish. With practice you'll adjust easily to the increased mass. Make sure you have a granny gear that's low enough, because there's no such thing as gearing too low for backcountry touring. Finally, check your brake pads. Stopping the increased weight will be hard on them.

Backpacks

Riding with a backpack eliminates the problem of weight distribution, although the pack may pull you rearward so you have to lean forward to compensate. Raising the handlebar may help by shifting the pack weight onto the waist belt, but on steep climbs this will overload your rear.

The best solution is to minimize total weight and use a pack that is carried as much as possible by the hips. Unfortunately, transferring weight to a hip belt is difficult in a bent-over riding position.

For singletracking, the freedom of movement afforded by a backpack is superior to riding with panniers. Bike handling is optimized, and you can easily lift the bike over a log or carry it across a stream. There is nothing to interfere with the bike's response on technical passages.

A side benefit of riding with a backpack is improved bike-handling skill. A backpack requires you to ride with a "quiet" upper body to prevent the weight from swinging. The quieter your upper body, the more precise your bike control.

 CREEK CROSSINGS

The three most important aspects of successful creek crossing are attitude, attitude, and attitude. If you want to graduate from being a rockhopper or log jumper to a certified creek crosser, you need a "go for it" frame of mind. You must be mentally prepared to pay the price of success (wet feet) or failure (wet body).

A little preparation goes a long way toward lessening the impact of a splashdown into the icy current. Clothing that can insulate when wet and is quick to dry is important. Also, tackling tough crossings when the weather is fair will help.

The second attitude that you must possess is a positive one. As Yoda said, "Do or do not, there is no try." You must believe that you can make it all the way every time; if you start with nagging doubts you will almost certainly fail.

Attitude number three is that when all else fails, remember that you are doing this for fun. Okay, you've just flown over the handlebar, you're drenched, and your bike is floating away. But hey, your friends got a great laugh, and if they'd been camera ready, your antics could have been immortalized. Are you having fun yet? Sure you are.

With the right attitude, you could probably make a go of it right now. But first, let's go through the following mental checklist.

Seat down: *Check!*
Toe straps loose: *Check!*
Fanny pack zippered tight: *Check!*
Positive attitude adjustment: *Check!*

The final prep is finding "the line." In some cases you can merely plow right through, especially if the creek bed is smooth. However, most mountain streams tend to be boulder strewn, so pick out a route through the path of least resistance. Often this means slowing down and studying the bottom while approaching. If it's boulder strewn and more than a foot deep, dismount and scout it.

Scouting might mean just a quick glance to see what's lurking below. Note whether the water is deep or the current swift.

Wetting Your Pants

Before you dive in, decide whether to take the slow, controlled approach or the hellbent for leather one. There are pros and cons to each. With the slow approach, you splash less and thus stay drier. If the weather's cold, this could be the deciding factor. And if you're forced to dismount, wet feet will probably be your only consequence. Most important, this method greatly reduces a novice's fear. The disadvantage of the slow method is limited momentum, which can disrupt forward progress.

Thus, the go for the gusto approach is generally best. The extra speed will power you over many obstacles that would stop the slow approach. This also makes for great photo opportunities. On the down side, if you do fall off your bike it's often spectacular. And whether you crash or not, you often get soaked to the bone.

Whichever approach you use, keep your weight back so the front wheel is less likely to be stopped by obstacles. If you let your body move too far forward, you'll set yourself up for an "endo."

Photograph 2-2. Keep your speed up and your weight back, and believe that you can make it all the way every time.

You want steady, continuous forward progress. Despite what you sometimes see in photos, don't lift your feet from the pedals to keep them dry. This sets you up for an accident of the worst kind. You need your feet secured for maximum balance.

After a few tries, you'll probably seek out creek crossings at every opportunity. However, no matter how addicted you become, know when to dismount and cross dry. For instance, consider a portage across a fast current or any creek that's strewn with logs or large rocks.

If you make many crossings, consider protecting your camera, tools, and lunch in Ziploc storage bags. A soggy sandwich will take the fun out of anyone's ride.

Proper clothing will make your ride afterward more bearable. Lycra is the most comfortable and quickest-drying material available. Also, wool socks are a must. As long as you're moving, your feet should stay warm with them. You might want to remove your shirt to keep it dry during a crossing, but if you don't, a polypropylene top will dry much faster than cotton.

If you cross streams regularly, learn to overhaul your hubs and bottom bracket. Check them after each ride involving long or deep water hazards. Also, remove your tires to drain water. If your tool kit is in your seat pouch, dry it before putting away your tools. Finally, it's time to jump in the shower and get wet all over again!

18 LOG JUMPING

You're on singletrack, darting around trees and rocks as you chase your friends. You're dialed in and having the time of your life until you spot a log across the trail. You see your friends disappearing and hope they rode around instead of over it, but soon you realize there is no alternative.

The log is about 8 inches in diameter, but the closer you get, the bigger it seems. Finally, your confidence runs out completely and you dismount. You lift the bike across and notice chainring scars on the bark. Remounting, you pedal off, but your rhythm is broken. You gain speed tenuously, half afraid that as soon as you get rolling again, another log will appear, which it does. It's about the same size as the first one, and you can see chainring scars on it, too. Your friends are nowhere in sight, and a corner of your mind still insists you can hop over it. But you don't.

That corner of your mind is right. All you have to do is hop the front wheel over the log. Don't worry about the rear; it will follow. It isn't very difficult.

First, learn to do a wheelie. Find a field clear of obstructions. Shift into your lowest gear. Relax. When you're ready, accelerate with a burst of power and yank back and up on the handlebar. The bike will pivot on the rear wheel, raising the front wheel off the ground. If done too weakly, the wheel will crash to earth after rising only an inch or two.

Try it again, but this time with more force. Accelerate hard and yank on the handlebar. The wheel will rise much higher this time—maybe so high that you'll start to topple backward and have to scramble to get your feet on the ground. That's good. You need to go to extremes to learn moderation. And moderation is the key to hopping over logs and rocks.

Your body's center of mass, roughly located in the abdomen, moves rearward in response to your lifting action. If this balance point moves so far back that it's behind the rear wheel's contact patch on the ground, you'll topple backward. If it remains in front of the contact patch, the front wheel will crash back to the ground. In a successful wheelie, your balance point is directly over the rear wheel's contact patch.

The only way to master a wheelie is through practice. But "wiring" wheelies isn't your goal. When you're confident you can lift the front wheel on demand, you're ready for a log.

Find a small one and set it in the field. Anchor the ends with dirt, sand, or rocks. Ride up to it slowly in your lowest gear. Just before the front wheel hits, accelerate hard and lift. Don't rush it or lift too high. All you need to do is clear the log and have enough momentum to drive the bike forward. As soon as the front wheel is back on the ground, start pedaling and the rear wheel will follow. Keep practicing until it comes naturally.

Of course, it's trickier in the woods, where the approach is likely to be narrower and bumpier. If the trail is level, focus on where you want to go. Ride up to the log or rock and smoothly loft the wheel. If you don't make it over the first time, try again. Keep practicing until you have it wired.

Over and Up

When you come to a log on a steep climb, you must modify this technique. There are two ways to unweight the front wheel. You can move your torso up and back as we've just seen, or you can suddenly lower it. To better understand these methods, stand on a bathroom scale. Now hop up without letting your feet leave the scale. You'll see your weight decrease, then increase before the reading settles back to actual body weight. To down-unweight, quickly bend your knees as if you're landing after a jump. You'll again see your weight momentarily decrease before increasing. Imagine the same basic move performed on a mountain bike and you'll understand the mechanics of down-unweighting.

Why is down-unweighting necessary? Because when climbing steep hills, the bike's front end is inherently light. This is why riders slide forward on the saddle or even crouch over the top tube. Throw your torso up and back to unweight the front wheel for a log and you're likely to topple backward.

Instead, drop your torso by flexing your arms (just as you did with your knees on the scale) while simultaneously lifting the handlebar. Practice until the movement feels right. Soon the front wheel will clear obstacles without affecting your balance.

A major advantage of this technique is that it positions the body beautifully for any ensuing moves. The bike's front end requires weighting for good steering response. Down-unweighting produces it. You're perfectly positioned to continue powering the bike forward and uphill. Just remember that you may need a rearward weight shift to maintain traction as the rear wheel goes over the log, especially if it's damp.

Down-unweighting is also done at speed when only a slight unweighting is needed rather than an actual lifting of the wheel. For example, if you're heading into a small depression and want to soften the front wheel impact on the upslope, down-unweight to absorb the bike's lift. You're actually absorbing the bike's upward movement with your arms rather than lifting its front end, but the result is the same.

Whether you up- or down-unweight, the trick is to do it fluidly. Always be aware of your center-of-mass relative to the bike, and lofting the front wheel over obstacles on climbs will be a snap.

Photographs 2-3, 2-4, 2-5. Once the front wheel is up and over the log, the rest of the bike follows naturally.

Over and Down

Unfortunately, it's different for hopping obstacles on steep downhills. This move is always challenging and somewhat intimidating. Normally the brakes are being applied. This and the gradient itself shifts weight forward. Consequently, unweighting the front wheel requires a severe weight transfer that opposes existing forces.

But one of these forces can momentarily be harnessed for help. Remember, before you can jump, your knees have to bend. The technique is to compress the front tire (as if it's a spring) by momentarily squeezing the front brake hard, then pulling up and back on the handlebar. Timing is tricky, but this technique works when the grade isn't too steep.

What makes the move intimidating is that if you blow the lift either by bad timing or insufficient height, the likelihood of flying over the handlebar is excellent. Or, if you succeed in clearing the obstacle, your acceleration may be so great that you grab the brakes just when the back wheel hits the log. The wheel bounces hard, your weight is shifted farther forward, the saddle smacks you in the butt, and over you go. Unfortunately, the only way to learn is to keep trying.

Another option is to move your butt behind the saddle and let the front wheel ride up and over the log. The trick here is to release the brakes just in time to let gravity pull you over. This way if the wheel doesn't clear, you'll just come to a stop—but without the dramatics of a forward air dismount.

19 THE BUNNY HOP

Using the bunny hop, riders can hop logs, rocks, ditches, curbs, cattle guards, you name it. It's a useful maneuver, but it takes a long time to learn and probably shouldn't be done too often, because it can be hard on bikes.

Nevertheless, bunny hopping and nailing the landing is exhilarating. One moment you're hammering the cranks, and the next you're flying over a curb or log that would have crushed your rim had you hit it straight on. Then the bike lands so smoothly you barely feel the impact. It's a buzz and a slick way to avoid unexpected obstacles.

Learning to hop is hard. You may have to work at it periodically for months before you can hop at will. Lofting the front wheel alone is easy; anybody can do it on the first attempt. But getting the back wheel into the air is tricky.

Flex, Then Pivot

There are two keys to the bunny hop. First, you must flex the bike hard before the jump. Second, you must pivot (or try to pivot) the handlebar forward.

Find an open field and a log about 4 inches in diameter. Place the log so you have a clear approach, landing, and runout. Bury the log's ends in sand or dirt so it won't move. Build a ramp out of hard-packed dirt on one side. Ride straight at it with some speed, and let the bike launch off the ramp. Your flight time won't be much, so don't get excited. What you're doing is learning to land the bike. Do it over and over until you're consistently smooth and confident.

Remove the ramp. But before you try jumping the log, ride slowly around the field. Suddenly press down hard on the front wheel, then yank it off the ground. Practice this until you can feel the tire actually bounce into the air.

When you're ready, circle back and ride straight at the log like before. Just before reaching it, compress the front tire hard, then hop it over. Don't worry about the back wheel yet; just let it bang into the log and bounce over. Repeat this maneuver until you feel confident doing it. The hard part is timing the compression and lift. When you can hop the front wheel as high as you want when you want, you're ready to learn how to hop the rear.

The Tricky Part

Again, ride slowly around the field. When going straight, squeeze the front brake hard and simultaneously pull up on the pedals with your feet (use toe clips and straps) as you twist the handlebar forward. Obviously, this has the potential to send you right over the bar, so be careful until you get the feel of it. Concentrate on the forward twisting of the handlebar and the lift with the legs. Practice until you can do a front-wheel wheelie on demand. Then try hopping the rear wheel without using the front brake. Practice until you've got it wired.

Photograph 2-6. Hopping is spectacular, but it also has practical applications.

Now you're ready to combine the two moves into one fluid, magical bunny hop. Go back to the anchored log. (You might want to use a smaller one if you're conservative.) Ride straight toward it at a speed you're comfortable with. Stand up, stop pedaling, compress the front tire hard, then jump as you simultaneously twist the handlebar forward and lift the pedals. If you're either a good learner or lucky, you just hopped the log. Congratulations.

More likely, however, your front wheel cleared the log with room to spare, but the rear hit it. Try again, but this time, before you compress the front tire, rotate your hands back by dropping your wrists. Now jump and twist the handlebar forward. Did you feel that? What a difference, eh? Felt almost as if the bike pivoted around the handlebar. By dropping your wrists before twisting hard, part of the energy that lifts the front wheel higher than necessary is transferred into lifting the back wheel.

If you didn't quite feel it, don't worry, just keep practicing. Unless you grew up on a BMX bike, it'll probably take a while. But you'll get it. Then you, too, can blast down trails and amaze your friends (and save your skin) by hopping stray logs, rocks, and ditches with the greatest of ease.

20 ADVANCED TRAIL TECHNIQUES

Once you've mastered the basics of mountain biking, use these off-road drills to increase your skill even more.

Skid turns. On a fast descent, you may need to simultaneously turn and reduce speed. This is done by intentionally locking the rear brake. To learn this technique, find a flat, smooth open area. While riding at moderate speed, stand on the pedals (cranks horizontal) with your weight back. Then tightly squeeze the rear brake lever and skid to a stop. Next, try applying pressure on the right pedal, which makes the rear wheel slide to the right (i.e., the bike steers to the left). Then try it in the opposite direction, applying pressure to the left pedal.

If you're careful, you can also experience the danger of locking the front brake. Ride slowly, balance your weight on the pedals, and squeeze the lever. You'll see that it's nearly impossible to keep the bike upright while the front wheel is skidding. Before long, you'll learn how much pressure can be applied to the front brake before it locks and you lose control.

Ruts. Cross a rut just as you would a set of railroad tracks—with your wheels perpendicular to it. If the rut isn't too deep, try riding in it. This teaches relaxation as it accustoms you to nonuniform surfaces (ruts often contain sand and gravel).

In shallow ruts, maintain enough speed to avoid bogging down. Let the bike steer itself. If the rut becomes too deep or narrow, shift your weight to the rear wheel and gradually stop.

Drop-offs. Never go over a drop-off without knowing what's below. If you're uncertain, stop at the edge and look.

If you decide to proceed, you must maintain some speed or you could go over the handlebar. Roll to the edge, tap the brakes if necessary, and descend with the front wheel perpendicular to the face of the drop-off. Simultaneously slide off the rear of the saddle and position your cranks horizontally. This allows the front wheel to touch down lightly, after which you can shift your weight slightly forward and roll to the bottom.

The steeper the drop-off, the more skill it requires. For example, if the face is vertical, you may need to slightly lift the front wheel rather than roll directly over the edge. Beginners should avoid drop-offs more than one foot high and heed this rule: When in doubt, dismount and walk.

21 PRACTICING AT HOME

Riding a mountain bike requires more skill than riding a road bike because trails present many different challenges, ranging from ruts, wash-outs, branches, and rocks to steep, twisting climbs and descents.

As the terrain changes, so must riding technique. You must apply power differently, brake differently, and anticipate new trail conditions. Your moves must become second nature, drawing upon upper-body strength, coordination, agility, and a precise sense of balance.

Surprisingly, one of the best places to develop these skills is your front yard. The following drills are fun, and they develop the talent necessary to perform well on your weekend trips to the trails. Practice them in the order listed for maximum development in minimum time. In case you fall, wear a helmet and protective clothing.

Up and over. To ride over an obstacle such as a log, rock, ledge, or rut, you need to lift the front wheel. Practicing on a curb will teach you how to balance the bike, transfer your weight, and apply power.

In a low gear, ride directly toward the curb at a steady, slow speed. When you're within 12 inches, lean forward to compress the front tire while positioning your dominant leg at the beginning of the power stroke (one o'clock for the right leg). As the wheel begins to rebound, simultaneously pull on the handlebar and push on the pedal. The front wheel will rise and clear the curb. As you feel the rear wheel make contact, lean forward slightly and your momentum will carry it over.

Make these movements smoothly. Beginners tend to yank on the handlebar, not realizing it's the combination of compression and leg power that lifts the wheel.

To ride off a curb or other barrier, hold the cranks horizontal while standing with your weight back to lighten the front wheel. Always keep your front wheel perpendicular to the obstacle.

Jumping. With every fast descent there's the risk of hitting a bump and becoming airborne, so it's important to learn how to land.

Use the incline where a driveway and curb intersect. Ride toward this spot from the sidewalk at a 30-degree angle, keeping two things in mind: First, stop pedaling before you begin a jump. Stand on the pedals with your weight slightly back, cranks horizontal. Stay relaxed and bend your knees to cushion the landing.

Second, always land on the rear wheel. If you should come down with your weight forward, you could lose control or even go over the handlebar.

After you learn to jump, don't practice too often. It's hard on a bike's fork, axles, bearings, and rims.

Steering through obstacles. On a trail, it's impossible to ride a straight line because of rocks and other debris. But if you learn to put objects "between your wheels" instead of riding completely around them, it will improve your bike control and help you maintain momentum on climbs.

To do this, place a can or paper cup on the street. Slowly ride toward it until your front wheel is a few inches away, then steer to the left or right. As soon as the wheel goes past, steer in the opposite direction so the rear wheel can pass on the other side of the object.

One-hand riding. At speed, most steering is done by shifting your weight, not by turning the handlebar. By practicing one-hand riding you will learn to use your whole body (especially your hips) to turn.

For this drill, choose a safe, flat area such as a yard or cul-de-sac. Ride progressively slower and make increasingly smaller circles, or do figure-eights around cans or cups. Alternate hands to develop a bilateral sense of balance.

Stationary balancing. Practice on an inclined driveway. Roll slowly into position perpendicular to the grade, brake to a stop, turn the front wheel toward the incline, and place the uphill-side pedal just above horizontal. To maintain balance, use pedal pressure to counter gravity's pull. Stay relaxed and don't use the brakes—you can't maintain balance unless the wheels are able to move slightly.

Part Three
BACKCOUNTRY SKILLS

∎22∎ WEATHER AWARENESS

Weather is beautiful. Weather is savage. Weather is thrilling. Weather is life-threatening. Above all, weather is largely indifferent to our existence. Mountain biking in the backcountry gives us a good chance to revel in the delights of our atmosphere, as long as we anticipate and cope with its threats.

In the Colorado Rockies, for instance, the wilderness seems benign. Poisonous snakes don't like the cool temperatures. The grizzly bear has been tragically eradicated. Bugs are inconsequential. Backwoods crime is almost unheard of. In Colorado, therefore, the primary problem in mastering the wilderness is coping with the weather. This can also be true in other parts of the country—sometimes when you least expect it.

Lightning Strikes!

Lightning is a special threat to mountain bikers because our metal vehicle conducts the electricity on its way to the ground. Lightning always looks for the shortest path to the earth, which means you must avoid high ground or isolated trees. Whenever lightning is possible, it's wise to scan the horizon before venturing into an elevated, open area. Are those towering, dark cumulonimbus clouds moving toward you or away from you? If toward you, find a lower route or wait out the storm. Summer showers often pass in just half an hour.

The Big Picture

You'll enjoy mountain biking more if you pause to watch the sky a little closer and are attentive to weather reports. This awareness of the grand patterns can really pay off in spring and fall, when big cyclonic low-pressure cells race across the continent, sometimes bringing continuous rain (and high winds or tornadoes) for days.

The sky can yield numerous clues to the future. For example, events in the upper atmosphere, where clouds are thin and wispy and jet aircraft leave contrails, can foretell weather in the next 48 hours.

Consider this weather pattern: It dawns clear, inviting you to venture into the backcountry to enjoy a day of riding. By 10:00 A.M. you notice cirrus clouds forming. By noon they cover half the sky. By 4:00 P.M. a broad sheet of cirrocumulus partially obscures the sun; the sky has turned from blue to white. At sunset the high cloud deck is set aflame by an orange sun shining on the horizon.

This sequence warns of an approaching warm front that could bring hours of rain beginning the next afternoon. Odds are that tomorrow will dawn with altocumulus clouds covering the sky. These will yield to stratus by noon and rain-bearing nimbus by three o'clock. Rain will continue all night.

Where can you learn this? From *Weather: A Guide to Phenomena and Forecasts,* by Paul E. Lehr and R. Will Burnett. It's an entertaining little book on a tremendously important aspect of our lives. And for more in-depth study, consider *A Field Guide to the Atmosphere,* by Vincent J. Schaefer and John A. Day, part of the Peterson Field Guide series. This book excels at explaining cloud types and the wonderfully varied patterns we see in the sky. It's loaded with photos, and the authors provide solid interpretations of every observation. Another good book is *Weathering the Wilderness,* by William Reifsnyder, a Sierra Club volume. The strengths of this book are its temperature tables, sunshine and precipitation information, and common storm patterns. It's organized by region.

A college-level introductory textbook on weather will make everything in the field guides and media reports far more understandable. Check your local college bookstore for *The Atmosphere: An Introduction to Meteorology* (4th edition).

Forecasting Services

In this day of satellites and instant global communication, the electronic media, especially television, provide the best weather information. Observations of cirrus clouds are fun and often provide useful knowledge, but they don't answer the critical questions: Will the wind blow hard and long enough to make my bike ride miserable? Will it stay cloudy for days, or will the front pass quickly? How extensive is the precipitation field?

Weather forecasting grows more accurate as increasingly powerful computers amass and assess greater amounts of data worldwide. So pay attention to the judgments of these professional forecasters.

National Weather Service (NWS). It issues several forecasts each day for regions in every state. Within a given region, however, terrain differences create microclimate variations. For example, the NWS Colorado Zone 4 forecast, "Central Mountains," includes Aspen, Crested Butte, and Leadville. Aspen gets more snow when the wind is out of the northwest. Crested Butte does better (they like snow) with the wind out of west-southwest. Leadville is on the other side of the Continental Divide and rarely gets as much snow as the rest of the zone. Thousand-foot elevation differences between each town create temperature variations of 3 to 5 degrees.

The Weather Channel. Available to cable TV viewers and satellite dish owners who have a Videocipher II descrambler, it offers moving satellite videos several times each hour. The company's on-screen personalities have good weather understanding and often try to explain complex weather topics. The display maps are above average. Approximately every 7 minutes the program broadcasts the NWS zone forecast.

A.M. Weather. This 15-minute TV program from the Public Broadcasting System airs Monday through Friday at 6:00 or 6:15 A.M. Despite its brevity, it provides a comprehensive picture of the weather in the lower 48 states.

Television news. Commercial TV broadcasters provide minimal explanation but use fantastic tools. The best is satellite imagery, especially the moving, 24-hour time-lapse videos with computer color enhancement. These can provide more information than any map or most forecasts.

NOAA Weather Radio. The NWS operates this radio network to broadcast local weather forecasts and information 24 hours a day. It's particularly useful for updates on the approach of severe weather, such as tornadoes, hurricanes, or blizzards. It uses high-frequency AM channels for which a special, inexpensive radio is required. Before buying one at your local radio/electronics store, be certain that NOAA broadcasts in your area.

Newspapers. Published forecasts are too infrequent, but at least you get some hard copy to study and think about.

On-line bulletin boards. With a personal computer and modem you can access local zone forecasts from Compuserve or other information services. Some cities have weather bulletin boards with an array of auxiliary information products. You can also subscribe to commercial weather computer systems, such as Accu-Weather in State College, Pennsylvania, or Weather Bank in Salt Lake City.

In addition to all of these professional forecasters, pay attention to your eyes, ears, nose, mouth, and skin. Electronics can never substitute for personal observations and conversations with locals. Our senses are a key to the enjoyment and understanding of our common heritage—the atmosphere.

∎23∎ MAP READING

Ever hear the old saw about a mountain biker being caught "up a trail without a map"? No? Well, it's only because creeks and paddles came first. Granted, no matter how well you know a creek, a paddle is still required, whereas well-marked trails (or those you've pedaled before) will lead you back home without a hitch. But who wants to ride the same trails all the time, or count on signs and markers for guidance in the backcountry?

Your ticket to exploration, of course, is a proper map. It's as essential to cycling the wilds as an air pump and water bottle. And, like the snake bite kit we toss into our panniers before a trip, it's best to know how to use one before you're in need.

Two Types

There are flat maps and topographic maps. The former is the type you get in service stations. It'll provide the critical information of distance and direction, but except for color shading to indicate mountain ranges, there are few clues about elevation gain and loss. Kansas and Colorado, for instance, look much the same. This isn't a problem if you're in a car. But on a bike? Pack food and water for a flat 30-mile trail and then encounter tough terrain, and you'll come home hungry and thirsty.

Many mountain bikers have therefore become as adept as backpackers at reading the second kind of map, topographic or "topo." These beauties are a cornucopia of information, such as detailed road classifications, trails, symbols of every-thing from footbridges and overpasses to dams and canals, and shadings to indicate swamps, wooded marshes, vineyards, and orchards. There's even a marking to tell you if a glacier is in the neighborhood. But best of all is what was missing from the flat map—elevation.

Topos indicate elevation with contour lines. Trace one with your finger and you'll know that every point on it is the same elevation. Contour lines are drawn in brown, and every fifth line is darker and marked with the altitude above, or depth below, sea level. The distance between the lines reflects the steepness of the terrain. Those spaced far apart depict relatively flat terrain; those massed together mean it's steep. The actual elevation change between lines (called the "con-tour interval designation") varies according to the map's scale.

Preride Any Trail

By reading contour lines, you can preride any trail in the nation. You can sit at your desk with a map and magnifying glass, picturing the route's deep canyons, hills, and mountain ridges.

If you plan a backcountry ride using a 1:62,500-scale map (i.e., 1 inch on the map equals 62,500 on the ground) with an 80-foot contour interval, you won't discover a brutal series of steep 79-foot hills until you're there. If you must know this information (e.g., you're planning to take some beginning riders), use the extremely detailed 7.5-minute or 1:24,000-scale map preferred by backpackers. The contour interval is usually 40 feet.

But the more detailed the map, the less area it covers. Hence, if you're riding on the flatlands and want to get the big picture, choose a 1:250,000-scale map with a contour interval of 200 feet, or the full-state 1:500,000 scale with a 500-foot interval. Full-state topos are recommended when planning long all-terrain tours that include off-road riding in widely separated locales. Supplement them with individual 7.5-minute maps for the trail-riding regions.

Topographic maps are available at many sports and outdoor specialty shops, bike shops, and for photocopying at public and university libraries. They can also be ordered. Ask for an index, price list, and the free instruction booklet, *Topographic Maps*. For areas east of the Mississippi River, including Puerto Rico and the Virgin Islands, write the U.S. Geological Survey, 1200 S. Eads Ave., Arlington, VA 22202. For locations west of the Mississippi, including Alaska, Hawaii, Louisiana, American Samoa, and Guam, write the U.S. Geological Survey, Box 25286, Federal Center, Denver, CO 80225.

24 COMPASS NAVIGATION

Maps and written instructions are usually sufficient to find your way. But there are times when even the most experienced backcountry biker can get lost, regardless of terrain.

Finding your way starts before you've lost it. Purchase a good compass, preferably one mounted on a clear "orienteering" baseplate. It's easier to hold, harder to lose, and possesses a scale along one edge for determining route distance. It will also help in determining your route in degrees.

The more sophisticated (and more expensive) units with mirror or see-through sighting lines provide slightly greater accuracy. And the needle in a sealed, fluid-filled compass "dances" far less than one suspended in air, thus enabling a quicker reading. However, a compass need not be expensive to be accurate.

Basic Directions

With compass in hand, you're straddling a bike wondering which of two trails to take. Most often, you'll simply consult your map, determine the preferred route to your objective, look at your compass to point you in the right direction, and begin pedaling.

However, if you're lost, or the trail you're on doesn't appear on the map, you should know how to take a bearing, or azimuth—the direction from you to some landmark, expressed in degrees.

For instance, if your destination is a lake, which is according to your map directly south of your present position (or where you think you are), perform the following actions with your baseplate compass.

1. Hold the compass level and in front of you, and face north.

2. Rotate your body so that the sighting line painted on the front of the compass baseplate faces south. In this case, the magnetic needle should be pointing directly at you.

3. Turn the compass dial until the inscribed arrow outline and the magnetic needle are perfectly aligned.

4. Follow the sighting line toward a landmark in the distance that's directly in front of it and start pedaling. Always keep the needle and inscribed arrow in perfect alignment and you can't go wrong.

As another example, if your destination is west, simply

face north in the direction of the magnetic needle, rotate your body 90 degrees to the left, and turn the compass dial so the arrow lines up with the needle. Finally, move in the direction you're facing, remembering to keep the needle and arrow aligned by rotating your body accordingly.

For a mirror compass, hold the unit at eye level and bend the mirror back toward you until the compass face can be seen through the window. The vertical hair in the window is your sighting line. Proceed as above.

Declination

There is one complication: the difference between magnetic and true north. Magnetic north is located in the region of Hudson Bay, while true north is the North Pole. These points are aligned only in relation to some parts of the country. If you're east of this "zero declination line," your compass will point west of true north; if you're west of it, the magnetic needle will point east of true north.

The problem is that maps are oriented to true north, while a compass needle points to magnetic north. Therefore, if you're in Salt Lake City and fail to adjust for this difference, you'll wind up 16 degrees east of your destination; in Maine you'll be 20 degrees west of your mark. To ease the problem, many compasses come with declination charts, and all topographic maps have a declination indicator for exact plotting.

Finally, with a topographic map you can take a bearing to a particular site without even being able to see it. Here's how.

1. Extend the magnetic north line on the map (located near the map scale).

2. Draw parallel lines across the map so one goes through your destination.

3. Lay the compass on the map so that your present location and your destination are intersected by the compass's side edge.

4. Rotate the dial so the inscribed arrow parallels the lines you've drawn. Your bearing is whatever degree the inscribed arrow points to. Just keep the magnetic needle and inscribed arrow aligned and you're heading in the right direction.

With practice, you'll get the hang of these basic techniques. You'll be glad you learned them even if you only use your compass occasionally to determine which of two or three possible trails to take. If you manage to save yourself just one arduous and time-consuming backtrack, I guarantee that a compass will be on your equipment list forever.

25 NUTRITIONAL ENERGY

If half the enjoyment is being there, the other half is getting there. And what makes the "getting there" part fun is a good attitude, proper training, and sound nutrition. The last is underscored by Dr. David Nieman, chairman of the Department of Health Science at Loma Linda University in California, who states that "proper nutrition ranks third behind talent and training in athletic endeavors."

While riding, your bike carries the weight, so the nutritional demands of a full day in the saddle vary little from individual to individual regardless of age, sex, or size. The energy needs for most of us fall somewhere between 4,000 and 5,000 calories per day.

The choice of fuel for your engine is the foundation of your physical performance. It's also the bedrock on which a healthy life is built. "Your diet," says Dr. Nieman, "should consist of 70 percent carbohydrate, 15 percent fat, and 15 percent protein." With diet so much in the news, most people know they should be eating fewer high-fat meats and dairy products, and more grains, cereals, potatoes, pasta, beans, brown rice, lentils, vegetables, and fruits. These carbohydrate-rich foods are also the best fuel for mountain biking.

Carbohydrate appears in food chiefly as sugars and starches. During digestion, these become simple sugars that are stored in the muscles and liver as glucose and easily burned for energy.

But our storage capacity is small. During a strenuous ride, blood sugar (and our energy) can drop dramatically in one hour. To keep it high, we must replace the sugar with a regular intake of complex carbohydrates. Easy-to-carry foods that work best are fresh fruits, raisins and other dried fruits, low-fat cookies (fig bars and oatmeal cookies), bagels, muffins, rice cakes, and energy bars.

Consuming a high-carbohydrate diet (i.e., 70 to 80 percent of intake) for several days before a trip can double your glycogen stores and maximize your performance potential. According to Dr. Nieman, this is "probably the most important nutritional principle for the fitness enthusiast and the endurance athlete to follow." Conversely, a low-carbohydrate diet can reduce available energy by 50 percent.

Like carbohydrate, protein provides 4 calories per gram. Protein also contains amino acids necessary for tissue maintenance. Major sources include eggs, dairy products, meat, fish, beans and peas, cereal, and nuts.

The average diet contains more than enough protein, and there's no evidence that extra amounts improve performance. In fact, excess protein is stored as fat.

As a long ride progresses, your body's main source of energy slowly switches from carbohydrate to fat. Unlike carbo, which is stored in limited supply, your reserve of fat is virtually endless. As you become more fit, your body learns to utilize its fat stores better. In fact, one reason top riders display such incredible endurance is that their bodies are fueled by the rich supply of body fat rather than the limited supply of carbohydrate.

However, this doesn't mean you should load up on dietary fats such as you'll find in ice cream, mayonnaise, cheese, meat, and nuts. You already have enough fat stored to last you for hundreds of hours of exercise. Thus, excess dietary fat adds only weight, not endurance. (A gram of fat contains 9 calories.) In addition, a fatty diet can contribute to heart disease, some types of cancer, and high blood pressure.

Once on the trail, calories are best utilized by eating and drinking about 20 percent of each day's requirement at each of the three meals, while consuming the remainder in the form of snacks and energy drinks.

For overnight trips, freeze-dried foods are still the most convenient and lightweight sources of energy. The freezing and water extracting processes have improved markedly in recent years. For instance, several manufacturers have taken a stand against preservatives and additives, producing a better-tasting and more nutritious pot of grub.

A few of your favorite spices can season freeze-dried foods to please. You'll never get the pleasure that comes from preparing meals from fresh ingredients, but for energy per ounce and ease of fixing, it's the way to go.

The Importance of Fluids

"The second most important dietary principle for individuals who exercise is to drink large quantities of water," says Dr. Nieman. Thirst is a sign that your body's fluid level is already low, so don't wait for the nag of a dry mouth to reach for refreshment. Dehydration is probably the most common health malady in mountain biking.

About 60 percent of your body is water, and this fluid is constantly being lost through perspiration, breathing, and urination. Water keeps the pressure balanced in and out of your cells, so you metabolize nutrients more efficiently and, therefore, have more energy. Your kidneys also need it to function properly; otherwise, some of their workload is delegated to your liver, and metabolism slows down still further. Also, lack of sufficient internal water may contribute to poor bowel activity, resulting in constipation.

The brain is very sensitive to water level changes, making dehydration one of the primary sources of outdoor headaches. With dehydration, your blood volume decreases, and you're a setup for the cold-weather problems of hypothermia and frostbite. In hot weather, water is required to keep the cooling perspiration mechanism running smoothly.

Besides thirst, fatigue, and headache, urine color indicates dehydration. It should be clear or light yellow; dark yellow or orange is a danger sign. Advanced indications of dehydration include light-headedness and increased heart rate, especially upon standing.

How much water do you need? On the average, 2 quarts per day. But a mountain biker can perspire away this much during just 1 hour of hard riding. To keep performance optimal, drink about 8 ounces of water every 15 to 20 minutes, or even more if it's hot.

When the sweat pours off, more than water is being lost;

electrolytes (sodium, chloride, potassium) are also excreted. Some commercial energy drinks offer a balanced electrolyte replacement with carbohydrate for fuel. As long as the sugar concentration isn't more than the 8 to 10 percent that causes a reduction in the rate at which the fluid is absorbed, they're a tremendous benefit. When mixing the powder with water, follow the label directions to ensure the proper proportions.

Since you can't pack all the water you need in the backcountry without becoming overburdened, carry a means of water purification such as halogen tablets (iodine usually works better than chlorine) or a filter (read the label to make sure it cleans out everything you want it to). Or carry a light camp stove to bring the water to a rolling boil.

Part Four
MEDICAL TIPS

26 YOUR PORTABLE HOSPITAL

The farther you wander from civilization, the more responsibility you have for ensuring your welfare. An essential component of that is the first-aid kit. Without one, no matter how skilled you are, you may be helpless when faced with an injury.

All first-aid kits are compromises. You must decide what level of preparedness is appropriate based on your first-aid knowledge and the nature of your exposure. The most common mountain biking injuries are cuts, scrapes, and bruises, with muscular and skeletal injuries next.

You can purchase a commercial first-aid kit, or build one like the following. For skin injuries, carry several sterile gauze pads, a gauze roll, tape, Band-Aids, an eye pad, and that wonderful Spenco product "Second Skin"—a gel-like substance. Also important are several butterfly closures for cuts more than ¼ inch deep or 1 inch long (they're also effective as emergency stitches).

To reduce the risk of infection, include a small vial of hydrogen peroxide, which kills germs and cleans the wound when water is unavailable or can't be trusted.

For sprains and strains, immediate application of cold reduces swelling and numbs pain. One option is to carry an instant cold pack. It's bulky but invaluable.

For muscle/ligament/tendon injuries, pack a triangular bandage, an Ace bandage (wide size), and heavy-duty tape. A broken bone requires immediate immobilization with a splint. You can make one using sticks, but a lightweight wire splint (1.75×30-inch) is better. They're available commercially, or you can make one from a roll of quarter-inch hardware cloth.

Preferred over-the-counter drugs are aspirin or ibuprofen. Either will diminish pain and reduce swelling. Another is Percogesic, which contains acetaminophen and a muscle relaxer, phenyltoloxamine. Which product to use is a judgment call.

Also carry vitamin E capsules for sunburn, rashes, and irritation. Packets of hydrocortisone can be helpful for poison ivy or poison oak and insect bites. Including decongestant pills doesn't hurt either.

A good pair of scissors is handy. Paramedics usually cut through clothing to get at wounds quickly without moving the victim. Safety pins are good for temporarily repairing the clothing. Tweezers for splinters are also useful. Carry moleskin for blister protection. And don't forget coins for an emergency phone call.

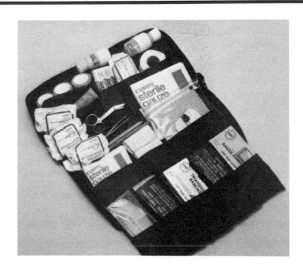

Photograph 4-1. First-aid supplies for the well-prepared rider.

An injured person lying on the ground loses heat fast. Hypothermia may be the primary threat to his or her life. You can't fit an emergency space blanket in a first-aid kit, but you can stuff one in your pack. Also include matches for starting a fire.

Except for the space blanket, all will fit in a 4-inch-diameter, 9-inch-tall stuff sack, but even that's too large. Therefore, a second, smaller kit is handy. That means prioritizing needs. For some people, the cold pack, bandages, tape, wire splint, elastic bandage, peroxide, and aspirin are most important.

If you decide to buy a commercial kit, Outdoor Research and REI both offer them in special nylon pouches. The Outdoor Research kits are well thought out and come in five sizes. The Mini omits treatment for a sprain or broken bone. The Basic and Compact kits are adequate, although the Basic omits butterfly closures. Both include four pill vials, perhaps too many. The Standard has all you'll need and more, but at 21 ounces will you take it with you? The Advanced is too extensive for mountain biking.

REI offers the 1st Essential and 1st Essential Lite at 22 and 12.5 ounces, respectively. The latter is minimal but adequate for most needs.

The REI and Outdoor Research kits lack the cold pack and wire splints, two important items. One solution is to buy Outdoor Research's Compact or Standard, or REI's 1st Essential Lite, then customize.

There's no consensus among authorities on the proper ingredients for a first-aid kit. But what's unanimous is the need to know how to use what you have. This requires study, formal or otherwise. Carrying a pocket guide is also helpful. One of the best is *Mountaineering Medicine,* by Fred T. Darvill, Jr., M.D., available at most mountaineering shops or from Skagit Mountain Rescue Unit, Inc., Box 2, Mount Vernon, WA 98273.

Any well-stocked pharmacy will have what you need to build a kit. REI also has a good selection of first-aid components in its stores, though unavailable by mail. Outdoor Research is at 1000 1st Ave. South, Seattle, WA 98134, (206) 467-8197. Also consider Mountain Medicine USA, Box 1478, Conway, NH 03818.

If you plan your portable hospital well, you could spare yourself a trip to an immobile one.

▮27 TREATING EYE INJURIES

Picking up speed on a coasting descent, a mountain biker's right eye smacks into an unidentified flying insect (UFI). The bug gets the worst of it, but with fat tires weaving across loose dirt, and one hand trying to pry open his irritated orb, the rider loses control.

Photograph 4-2. "Mud in your eye" is a reality for mountain bikers —and it's only one of the potential hazards.

The next morning, mismatched organs of sight stare back at him from the mirror, one white and one red. The red one hurts. With rest and warm washes, this problem, too, is soon over. But the accident and the inflammation are potent reminders. He'll never forget his safety glasses now when he rides.

Your eye is a delicate Ping-Pong ball, of which only a small slice is visible to the outside world. The ball is full of a jellylike substance, the vitreous humor. A window in front, the cornea, allows light to enter the eye. The cornea covers a slight bulge in the ball that's filled with a salty fluid. Between the bulge and the ball lies the lens. Over the lens is a special muscle, the iris, which has an adjustable opening, the pupil. Working together, they focus images on the retina, a layer of sensitive cells that covers the back of the eye. Translated into electrical signals and carried by the optic nerves from each eye to the back of the brain, the image is decoded into thought.

Because it is delicate, your eye is protected in several ways. The outside of the ball, except over the cornea, is covered with a tough membrane called the sclera, the "white" of the eye. A thin mucous membrane, the conjunctiva, covers the exposed part of the eye and the inner side of the eyelid. Tear glands keep the eye moist, washing out most of the dust and debris. The eyelids add protection and help sweep the surface of the eye clean when you blink. A bony socket surrounds the Ping-Pong ball with a protective shield. It's lined with fatty "shock absorbers," a final barrier against physical abuse.

Foreign Bodies

Undoubtedly the most common threat to a cyclist's eyes is when something gets in there that doesn't belong: usually mud, dirt, or bugs. The discomfort can be enormous, but often the victim's tearing mechanism will wash the eye clean in time. Good first aid is simply to try to avoid rubbing the eye and to wash it with copious amounts of clean water.

Irrigation is best done by laying the patient down and emptying a water bottle on the bridge of his or her nose. Rapid blinking encourages the flushing process.

There's no harm in gently removing large chunks of debris from an eye with the moist tip of a tissue or bandanna, but there are two exceptions:

- Do not try to force out anything that seems stuck.
- Do not try to remove anything lying on the surface of the cornea.

If additional rinsing doesn't work, cover the eye with a folded gauze pad or sterile eye patch and tape it shut. Find a doctor.

Sometimes the eye feels irritated after the foreign bodies are removed. The patient may complain of pain when he blinks. Probably the eye has suffered an abrasion. If the problem continues after another washing, patch the eye shut. Pain might be relieved by an anti-inflammatory analgesic like ibuprofen (Advil, Nuprin, and others). Do not apply a topical anesthetic without a physician's guidance. It can slow healing, inhibit protective reflexes, and even harm tissue in the eye. Irritation that persists for 24 hours is encouragement to seek a hospital.

Impaled Objects

In the worst-case scenario, a twig or other sharp object punctures the eyeball. If the object is still there, do not try to remove it. But whether it's there or not, keep the patient lying down. Gravity can be either a friend or foe in keeping the jellylike substance in the eye. This is critical to sight.

It's necessary to stabilize the impaled object. One way is to make a "doughnut" out of a rolled bandanna. Place it gently around the eye. Next, put a cup over the donut so nothing can catch or jar the object. Then, tape it all down securely, and also patch the other eye shut. If the good eye looks around nervously, the bad eye will try to follow and more damage can be done. The patient must be carried to a hospital. This is a good time to remain calm and speak reassuringly.

Contusions

You can call this oneperiorbital ecchmyosis to impress your friends, but if you say "black eye," a universal understanding will prevail. The owner of the shiner may be anxious over the rapid swelling and discoloration; the white may turn an alarming red. A cold compress will reduce the pain and swelling. It takes 12 to 24 hours for the swollen eye to look relatively normal in size, but a week to ten days is required for the discoloration to clear.

Acceptable reasons for panic after a poke in the eye include:

- Persistent blurred vision
- Persistent double vision
- Extraordinary sensitivity to light
- A discharge of something other than tears

These problems require professional medical attention.

Lacerations

A slice in the lid tends to produce a lot of blood because of the richness of the supply to this area. Relax and check the eyeball for a cut. A lacerated eyeball means the patient must be kept still and lying down with both eyes patched. Otherwise, cover the wound with a light, sterile dressing. Although the slice may be quite small, a scar on the eyelid can be a discomfort for the rest of your life. An expert can stitch the wound neatly closed with little or no noticeable scarring.

Infections

An infected eye is red, and it burns, itches, tears, and generally produces unhappiness. The problem will usually resolve itself, but warm compresses often give relief. If the eye produces a large amount of a purulent discharge (pus), or if the eye is sealed shut with a hard crust, it's time to seek medical advice. In the meantime, do not patch this eye closed. It needs to drain. If the eye swells, accompanied by increasing pain and a fever, stop the warm compresses. Instead, apply cold to the eye and find a doctor.

If it comes to a vote on whether to wear protection, let's hope the eyes have it.

▪28▪ DEALING WITH HEAD INJURIES

In places the asphalt was clean, but on the bridge the cold New Hampshire night had left a sheet of invisible ice. She pedaled along furiously, anxious to get to the head of the trail, anxious to heat up the cold morning with activity. Her hair was hidden under a heavy wool cap, the kind with ear flaps—great for warmth, but not for impact protection. Witnessing the fall from several bikelengths behind, her friend said he could hear the thud of her head as it struck the curb.

When the ambulance arrived, her eyes were swollen shut and she was mumbling incoherently. Thick fluid leaked from her nose. She irritably pushed at rescue workers' hands as they moved her to the restraints of a spineboard. Though she was unable to stand, her restless movements might have caused even more serious injury.

A helicopter sped her to Boston, where surgery relieved the pressure on her brain, but it was several months before she fully recovered. Her memory of the accident and the next couple of days has never returned. She was fortunate to have rapid evacuation available. The often subtle and serious complications of a severe head injury usually cause death in as little as 4 hours.

The bulk of your brain is the cerebrum, the gray matter, the center of higher functions like thought and emotion. In the back of your head, beneath the cerebrum, is the cerebellum, where equilibrium and coordination are controlled. The brain stem grows from the base of the brain and is responsible for vital involuntary functions, including circulation and respiration. Enclosing the brain and spinal cord are three blood-rich layers of tissue, which from the brain outward are called the pia mater, arachnoid, and dura mater; collectively they're the meninges. Cerebrospinal fluid (CSF), which constantly fills the spaces between the meninges and washes the brain and spinal cord, is a clear liquid that protects and feeds the central nervous system.

Your brain sits about 1 millimeter from the inside of your skull, comfortably in command of everything that goes on in your body—if the temperature, salt, water, blood sugar, and pressure within your head remain balanced. Head trauma ranges from simple scalp abrasion to severe brain damage. The severity is usually a result of the uncompromising structure of the skull or cranium. If the brain starts to swell it will be squashed, because there's no room for swelling to take place.

Brain injuries can be loosely divided into these categories.

1. No loss of consciousness. Rarely does this result in a serious problem, despite sometimes heavy bleeding and a huge goose-egg-size bump. The brain has not been damaged.

2. Mild or short-term unconsciousness. A concussion reveals that the victim's brain briefly contacted the inside of the cranium and some transient loss of function occurred. There's usually nothing to worry about. The victim may be unaware of having been unconscious. Ask witnesses, if possible. Watch for the following telltale signs of increasing intracranial pressure (ICP):

- Headache that increases in intensity
- Blurred vision or other visual disturbance
- Level of consciousness that generally progresses from disorientation to irritability to combativeness to comatose
- Heart rate that slows and starts to bound
- Breathing that becomes noticeably irregular
- Skin that becomes flushed and warm, especially in the face
- Pupils that become unequal in size

3. Long-term unconsciousness. This is a serious warning that ICP may be on the rise. The problem may be a bruise to the brain, a tear in the blood vessels of the meninges, or a laceration of the brain itself. The tough dura mater clings to the inside of the cranium. Blood collecting between the dura and the cranium is called an epidural hematoma. A subdural hematoma is blood between the dura and the brain. The blood can gather over hours or weeks, increasing the pressure until death.

Obvious signs of head injury include a depressed spot where the skull is fractured, visible fracture lines where a portion of the scalp has been torn away, black-and-blue marks around swollen eyes or behind and below the ears, and blood or clear cerebrospinal fluid (or both) weeping from the nose or ears. Seizures are common.

Don't wait for these danger signals. Seek professional medical attention for anyone knocked unconscious.

Move the injured patient gently to prevent damage to the spinal cord, which is often at risk from a severe blow to the head. Such damage will prevent the chin from dropping to the chest. Keep the patient lying down. If the ground slopes, his head and shoulders should be uphill. If he slips into a coma, monitor closely to make sure his tongue doesn't fall back across his airway. If the patient must be left alone, roll him carefully on his side to keep the airway open. Be aware that head-injured people, whether conscious or not, are likely to vomit.

Once in the hospital, even the seriously injured patient has a good chance to survive. Oxygen therapy, drug therapy, and surgical intervention are available. One objective is to keep the patient awake or arouse him regularly. But in the backcountry, let your patient sleep if he wants to. During sleep, the brain has the best chance to control its own swelling. If the patient is showing signs of improvement after 48 hours, his prognosis is good.

As long as roads and trails beckon and folks pedal freely where wind is the only common visitor, heads will be injured. Wearing a helmet is the primary method of prevention. But even severe accidents need not lead to tragedy if rescuers use their heads.

29 TREATING SPRAINS AND STRAINS

Green. So fresh, so fine, it blurred the distance in a vernal mist. Up close, the new buds paled, while the trees looked mostly winter brown. But the snow was gone—the leaves were matted to the ground from their recent burial, and the air was hard and sweet. It was too perfect a day to stay inside.

David chose the old cross-country ski trail to ride. There's a pitch where the creek jumps off a rock face and you have to portage your bike, but otherwise the ride is long and relatively flat, and just right for getting back into the mountain biking mode. David was alone again, as he often preferred.

Tired, a bit out of shape, he pushed too hard on the return run to asphalt. A half mile out, where the trail corners, he lost traction in a patch of wet leaves. When he threw his right leg out for support, his ankle rolled and exploded in pain. He tried to stop the ground from coming up so fast, but something popped in his right wrist. For a few moments he lay on the soggy carpet, wishing his ankle belonged to someone else.

The most immediate question was, "How serious is it?" Probing around the joint with his healthy hand, David found nothing that said broken bone: no unusual movement, no numbness or tingling in his foot, no exceptional feeling of cold, nothing to distinguish one ankle from the other except the pain.

Strains, sprains, fractures, and all serious musculoskeletal injuries have one thing in common—they make the affected limb too painful to use. But intuitively, David trusted his ankle. It worked and so did his wrist, so he rode out slowly. At home, he ripped into a cold beer and soaked in a hot bath.

Next morning, the swelling and discoloration would have made his own mother turn away. He could only hobble painfully to work, and his wrist wouldn't even support a cup of wake-up coffee. Mismanagement had turned a minor injury into a big problem. Almost a year after the accident, David complained of the soreness in his right ankle.

A fracture needs a splint, a trip to an emergency room, an x-ray, a cast, and a few weeks or months to heal permanently. A strain (torn muscles) or a sprain (torn ligaments) can bother us the rest of our lives if we treat it improperly. What's really unfortunate is that these injuries don't hurt as much as they should. Pain would encourage us to act sensibly, meaning first aid, rest, and retraining.

RICE

Our first response is critical. Every minute RICE is delayed can add an hour to healing. RICE is an acronym for Rest, Ice,

Compression, and Elevation. Stay off the injured limb for the first half hour while you reduce its temperature as much as possible without freezing. Crushed ice is best because it conforms to the shape of the anatomy. Don't put the ice directly on your skin. This could produce a cold injury. Instead, cover the ice with a shirt or towel.

If ice is unavailable, soak the afflicted area in a mountain stream or use the chemical cold pack from your first-aid kit. During warm months you can wrap the joint in a wet T-shirt and let evaporation cool the area.

Compression requires an Ace-type bandage. Placing spare socks around the injury beneath the bandage keeps the compression more uniform. Wrap the limb snugly, but watch it carefully for loss of circulation, tingling, numbness, or pain caused by overaggressive compression.

Elevation means keeping the injured limb higher than the heart. After RICE, let rewarming occur before trying to use the joint, in order to prevent further damage facilitated by the ice-induced anesthesia.

The goal of RICE is to limit swelling. The more the injury swells, the less you can move the affected area. The less you move, the quicker the muscle deteriorates and the longer it takes to heal. During the next 48 hours, use the injured limb as little as possible, maintain compression, and apply ice three or four times per day.

As soon as the swelling stops, start exercising the joint. Wiggle it gently, spell the alphabet in the air with your toe or finger, and add mild heat to loosen the stiffness—but no more than a few degrees above body temperature. If swelling begins to increase, return to cold. But continue the exercising as much as pain allows. You're increasing circulation to carry off the excess fluid and dead cells surrounding the injury. This smooths out the fibers of the ligaments and strengthens the muscles, thus speeding healing.

Even a mild sprain may take two months to heal solidly. You may be comfortable in one week and feeling marvelous in two, but don't be fooled. Exercise your injured joint aggressively but not past the point of pain. If you're worse the next day, retreat and push forward more gently.

Mountain biking is an excellent way to retrain a sprained ankle, especially if you use toe clips. A mountain bike can be great exercise for sprained knees, too. Stay on pavement, though, to avoid jarring and pounding. Roll your ankle slowly through a full range of motion with the clips. As more strength is developed, a higher level of activity can be attempted.

How do you know when you're well? Test your joints independently, increasing the pressure on them slowly. Is your balance the same? How about your strength? Does the injured side hurt while the healthy side doesn't? Hop a few times on the sprained ankle. If you can't, you aren't completely healed. When your strength and pain responses are bilaterally equal for approximately ten repetitions of the same movement, you're ready to increase your training schedule.

Shoulders, elbows, wrists, fingers, knees, ankles, and toes can all be sprained, and the supporting muscles can be strained. The principles for treatment don't change with the body part. You'll need a RICE period, rest period, and retraining period. But stretching and strengthening should be specific to the injured area.

Remember to ride the road to recovery with the same vigor and discipline you give to the activity that produces your injuries . . . and your well-being.

30 WATER IN THE WILD

The subject in question was the little pond near the top of Oak Hill. The riders' bikes lay in early grass. The hill was low and unassuming, but lovely and far from pavement. The grunt uphill had caused them to drink their bottles dry. "Yeah," one said. "I don't see anything funny in there."

"What you can see is not going to hurt you," says Dr. Steven Sell, author of *Water Purification in the Wild.* Not exactly true, of course, but his point is that "illnesses that usually result from drinking bad water are caused by what you can't see."

Two days after drinking the Oak Hill water, one rider had a severe diarrheal episode lasting about 6 hours. Another had no severe trouble but shared her suffering (a little). Both cursed the beavers that had probably traveled miles out of their way to infect the pond.

There's only one way to know if something is homesteading in your intestinal tract: have a stool sample tested. Otherwise, the final verdict on what caused the diarrhea is difficult to obtain. Of the sufferers who blame their discomfort on backcountry water, many test positive for campylobacter, salmonella, and shigella. Dr. Sell states that worldwide only about 2 percent will test positive for the dreaded *Giardia lamblia.*

Giardia is a flagellate protozoan transmitted to water as a cyst in the feces of infected mammals. Undoubtedly, man is the chief disseminator in remote areas. If an estimated 25 to 50 cysts penetrate the body, they hatch, reproduce, and colonize in the ideal warm and moist environment of the small intestine. The colony usually grows for 12 to 15 days before obvious signs of trouble appear, but in some individuals, incubation can extend to 75 days. You can't return from a weekend trip with giardia unless you swallowed the creatures at least a weekend earlier.

Giardia causes a foul diarrhea that lasts from one to several weeks. Abdominal rumbling and distention produce uncomfortable cramps and a putrid gas that will determine who your friends are. Fatigue and weight loss are usual; fever and vomiting are not, but they may occur in the first day or two after symptoms appear. It's rare for giardia to be life-threatening, although you may wish you were dead.

Treatment

Diarrhea from unpotable water ends when the body has rid itself of the cause. The greatest danger lies in the fluid and electrolyte loss that accompanies the purging process. Protection requires 4 to 5 quarts of liquid per day in solution with a pinch of salt and a tablespoon of honey or sugar. If baking soda is available, a teaspoon in every other quart will encourage electrolyte replacement. Potassium is also important in treating prolonged diarrheal illnesses. Clear fruit juices, even powdered, will do the job. Mixing a diluted solution of electrolytes such as Gatorade works fine, so keep a few packets in your first-aid kit.

Also stock tablets of bismuth subsalicylate (Pepto-Bismol) for symptomatic relief, but not if you are intolerant of aspirin.

A new over-the-counter drug that's equally effective as a liquid cork is Imodium.

Drugs that stop normal bowel activity keep the annoying life forms trapped inside the patient's body and hence should be used with discretion. There are also prescription medications to shorten the lives of your uninvited intestinal guests.

When is the problem serious? Most diarrhea will self-limit within 24 hours. A painful, watery diarrhea that persists and drives you to the bushes 10 or 12 times each day requires a physician. Fever and bloody stools often indicate a bacterial pathogen that also demands aggressive medical treatment.

There's probably no such thing as clean water anymore. The Safe Drinking Water Act of 1974 allows the liquid that runs out of your tap to contain up to 200 colonies of coliform bacteria in every 100 cubic centimeters of water. Coliforms flower in your intestinal tract naturally, so high counts in water indicate contamination with human waste. If this constitutes safe water, then off-road sources often may be comparatively harmless.

The best sources of safe groundwater are springs and streams that descend from high uninhabited areas. Look for sources that run at right angles to the long axis of the valley. Water that runs smoothly tends to be safer than a tumbling torrent. Churning action stirs up organisms like giardia from the bottom; otherwise they sink. Unfortunately, any sip of water from today's earth is a gamble with disease.

Prevention

The only way to reduce the risk of infection is to disinfect the water. Giardia in its cyst and free-swimming form will die instantly when water is heated to 140° to 160°F. A Wilderness Medical Society position paper offers this rule of thumb: "A rolling boil at any altitude in North America will kill giardia." Although most bacteria will die along with the giardia, many viruses are resistant and need more heat for a longer period.

Water can be disinfected chemically, but this method's effectiveness is altered by water temperature, pH, and clarity. The colder and dirtier the water, the more reagent is needed for a longer period. If a suspension of organic matter muddies the water, adding about three pinches of alum per quart greatly speeds the settling process. Iodine is more reliable than chlorine and easier to carry and use. Given time to act, iodine will kill anything (including you) if the dose is too high. If you choose a commercially prepared iodine, follow the directions on the label. A tincture of 2 percent available iodine is effective at 8 to 16 drops per quart (depending on temperature) and after a 30-minute wait.

Filtration can clean your water if the filter is designed to remove what you want removed. A useful filter has a screen with tiny holes and an activated charcoal element. But no matter how expensive, it won't remove ultramicroscopic viruses.

If you suffer an acute attack of diarrhea that's short lived, it's probably viral. A longer episode with fever is most likely bacterial and requires treatment with an antibiotic. A prolonged illness may be giardia. None of these is fun. So when the backcountry calls, be sure to carry an adequate water supply or the means to disinfect it.

Part Five
ODDS AND ENDS

31 YOUR FIRST MOUNTAIN BIKE RACE

Anyone who has raced on a road bike remembers their first time in a large pack. A one-word description might be "terror." There's a sudden realization that this isn't a training ride. Nobody's going to politely move over and let you into the paceline. And even if you were physically equal to the others, you almost certainly fell victim to some elementary tactic and missed the winning break.

Deciding to race a road bikc is not a lighthearted choice. You can't really "run what ya brung," because only a first-class machine will keep you in the pack. If you don't have team-mates and a support crew, a flat tire will put you out of contention. And, finally, road racing is tough and calls on all your reserves. It's only fun if you can stay with the field. If you're "off the back," you might as well turn around and go home.

Road racing is also a sport where the spectator realizes he can't hope to match his riding skills with the pros any more than a baseball fan can hope to hit "Smoke" Stewart's fastball.

In contrast, mountain bike racing is a participatory sport that's comparable to recreational foot races. It isn't unusual to see entire families competing. The family members don't need to have fancy bikes, they don't need to wear fancy cycling clothes, and they can't all stay with the leaders. But they do seem to have fun.

Mountain bikers race for many reasons. The riders in front are seasoned and competitive athletes who are trying to win, but trailing them by as much as half an hour is a collection of enthusiasts who just want to beat a cousin, or set a personal best, or try out a new bike. There are as many reasons as there are "recreational competitors."

Get Ready. . .

If you want to compete in a mountain bike race, begin by preregistering by mail. This usually saves a few bucks, but mainly it's to beat the rider limit. There's no guarantee you'll be allowed to enter just because you show up on race day. You'll also need a license. To get one, contact the National Off-Road Bicycle Association (NORBA), 1750 E. Boulder St., #4, Colorado Springs, CO 80909.

Two elements that will contribute most to your success are fitness and bike preparation. If you don't train hard before the race you'll still have fun . . . it'll just take longer. And one of the best training methods for mountain bike racing is road riding, because you can maintain a high cadence for long periods. However, this doesn't require a road bike. You'll be racing on your mountain bike, so use it for all your training.

Although road riding will increase your speed and endurance, off-road training will improve your handling skills and strength. Climbing in the dirt is especially important. To paraphrase an old proverb, a mountain bike race is not to the swift as much as it is to the good climber.

Remember also that mountain bike racing is largely a time trial. It has few of the tactical elements of road racing, which are based on the effect of the wind on large groups of cyclists moving at high speed. In time trials, mental strength and the ability to pace yourself are assets, because it's hard to monitor your progress against the competition.

Get Set. . .

Prepare your bike carefully before the race. This may be obvious, but even the best riders fall victim to inadequate mechanical prep.

Check the tightness of each nut. Oil the chain and derailleurs. Inspect the cables for wear and proper tension. Check tire inflation. Adjust brake pad position. Make sure you have a spare tube and pump. Don't expect to be able to fill your water bottle at the starting line; instead, fill several before the race.

Go!

The hairiest part of a mountain bike race is the start. In the beginner and intermediate classes there are often 100 or more riders in the same event. Sometimes it can take 5 minutes for the entire group to get moving. Until distance and hills string things out, it can be crazy. If the course is dry, the riders will kick up so much dust that you won't be able to see what you're riding over. If it's wet, mud in your eyes or on your lenses will cause the same result. Invariably there will be a few entanglements accompanied by industrial language.

As soon as there's a hill or technical section, the mob will slow and disperse. At first, your race position will depend on your luck in getting a good start. But as soon as there's room, the faster riders will begin to move ahead. Etiquette requires that you let a faster rider pass. If you dismount on steep hills, allow those still riding to pass so they don't lose momentum. When overtaking another rider, it's unwise to shout, "On your left!" because half the time your exhausted opponent will think it's a suggestion and move that way. Instead, give adequate warning, then react to his or her movements.

Despite the media glorification of airborne cycling, resist the temptation to launch yourself off every rock, particularly if you're unfamiliar with the course. Your bike is under control only when its tires are on the ground. It's silly to lose a race or damage your bike by showboating for the crowd.

Watch out for spectators, especially on descents. When you enter a fast corner and see a crowd, it's a sure sign of a surprise ahead. Crowds tend to form where riders go down. You know you're in trouble when you hear a collective groan about 2 seconds before you crash.

Try to ride within your handling skills, although you'll be tempted to exceed them. If you're left behind on a descent by a clearly superior rider, don't try to keep up, just ride your pace. Otherwise, set your sights on the rider just ahead and reel him in. Of course, someone behind has you targeted for the same thing, so keep an eye there, too.

Whoa!

The most dangerous moment will be immediately after you finish. Resist the temptation to slide into a flashy 180-degree stop so you can wave to all your friends who beat you. For some reason, riders tend to lose concentration when they finish, and a high percentage of these final gestures end with a crash in front of the delighted crowd. The most memorable was pro rider Roy Rivers "spiking" himself like a football at the finish of the 1985 NORBA Nationals.

The best part of the event is the après-race celebration when riders replenish body liquids and dissect the race. You'll hear 15-minute descriptions of things that took 2 seconds to occur and every excuse for poor performance known to cycling science.

And herein lies the main difference between the two types of competitive cycling: Road racing is like a real sport, but mountain bike racing, for most participants, is like a 25-mile party.

◼32 MOUNTAIN BIKE FESTIVALS

Mountain bikers are, by nature, gregarious types, and their sport has spawned a phenomenon that has no counterpart in the cycling world—the fat-tire festival. Although other recreational cyclists gather in large groups, a club century or a Ride Across The Great State of Somewhere (RATGASS) just isn't the same.

There is no such thing as a typical fat-tire festival, since every promoter and each area lends unique qualities to the gathering. Some festivals feature lots of racing; others, none at all. Some offer carefully organized rides; others thrive on spontaneity. Some last for a week; others, a weekend. Simply put, there is no set of criteria that makes an event a festival. If the promoter says it's one, then it must be. A couple hundred mountain bikers can't be wrong.

Fat fests do have a few things in common, though. For instance, most are the largest gathering of mountain bike riders ever witnessed in the area. Every car has a bike rack. Every conversation focuses on a single theme (and it isn't football). Every bike shop does a brisk business. And every restaurant in town has to set up tables for parties of 15 to 20 exuberant diners who eat everything but the table.

For new mountain bikers, there are usually nonthreatening groups to cycle with and learn from. At some festivals there are even "women only" rides, which are free of the macho mentality that some females find intimidating. For more experienced cyclists looking for new challenges short of racing, there's the opportunity for fast recreational rides with some of the sport's emerging legends—everyone from well-known framebuilders to national champions. Even famous roadies have been known to show up for a little R&R at some fall festivals.

If you haven't been to one of these events and it sounds like a good time, you're only half right. You'll have twice as much fun as you imagine. Here's a sampling of the best-known fat-tire festivals.

Fat-Tire Bike Week
Crested Butte, Colorado

This was the first of the fat-tire festivals, and for a few years it was the only one. Crested Butte (elevation, 9,000 feet) is an old mining town that's surrounded by picturesque Rocky Mountain peaks, some taller than 12,000 feet. The Butte lures skiers to the nearby slopes during winter and attracts tourists in the summer. Ten years ago just the main street was paved.

FTBW, which is pronounced "Bike Week," had its roots in

the now famous Crested Butte-to-Aspen ride over Pearl Pass, a spontaneous local event that began in the fall of 1976. Since this was before mountain bikes were even invented, these off-road pioneers just used old bikes. In 1978, five Californians traveled to Crested Butte to take part, and although the numbers were small, the sport's first festival had been born.

Indeed, FTBW was a regular event on the cycling calendar before those involved even realized it. Every year the number of riders grew—from 13 in 1978, to 30 the next year, to 90 the year after that, to 300 in the peak years of 1982 and 1983. Since it's a long way to Crested Butte from anywhere, those who came wanted more than one ride. In fact, cyclists soon started arriving a week early for other rides before the biggie.

Photograph 5-1. Fat-Tire Bike Week in Crested Butte, Colorado, features everything from mass-start recreational rides and races to bicycle polo.

Luckily, facilities existed to handle large numbers of skiers, and these were underutilized during the fall. The locals quickly realized the slow-season potential of this new sport, and the entire town caught fat-tire fever. Soon there were bike expos, observed trials contests, races, and dozens of recreational rides. There's even a Mountain Bike Hall of Fame and Museum with an annual induction ceremony. In 1988, the first group of inductees included Tom Ritchey, Gary Fisher, Joe Breeze, Jacquie Phelan, Charlie Cunningham, Mike Sinyard, Joe Murray, Steve Cook, Neil Murdock, and Charlie Kelly. More fun than formality, the induction party is a chance for everyone to meet the people who shaped the sport. The museum itself houses some of the oldest and most influential of the original mountain bikes, as well as articles and photos from the sport's seminal era.

For more information, write Crested Butte Fat-Tire Bike Week, Box 782, Crested Butte, CO 81224.

Canyonlands Fat-Tire Festival
Moab, Utah

Moab, which is near the junction of the Green and Colorado rivers, has become the site of another famous mountain bike festival. In fact, the Canyonlands Fat-Tire Festival is threatening to eclipse the one in Crested Butte.

Perhaps the biggest reason is its proximity to major travel routes, compared to the remoteness of Butte. (Amtrak stops an afternoon's bike ride up the road, and Moab is just south of Interstate 70 on U.S. 191.) Moab is also the gateway to Canyonlands National Park, a vast tract of river-cut sandstone and spectacular views that has become popular for mountain bike touring. (The Canyonlands is an arid area, and visitors are required to register at the park office in Moab and carry adequate water.)

The weather also contributes to Moab's popularity (the high mountains are beautifully snow-capped by late October), as do such unique traditions as an annual Halloween party where all the costumes are bicycle related. (One year a memorable attendee, labeled the "Off-Road Warrior," sported a helmet with a crest made from a tire.)

Moab's fat fest has roots in motorcycling, an association most mountain bike riders would rather forget. Before bicyclists discovered the unique sandstone formations known as the slickrock, motorcyclists had mapped the Slickrock Trail. It's indicated by painted dots that wind through the landscape of smooth, rounded rock.

Despite its name, the traction afforded by this surface is great. Still, negotiating the slickrock is challenging. There are ample opportunities for accidents, ranging from skinned knees (common) to fatal cliff dives (none to date). Riding with semideflated tires for maximum stickiness is the local style, and many experts prefer slick tread. To give you an idea of how tough it is, an accomplished rider can usually finish the 12-mile course in about 2 hours. For others, it can take 4 to 5 hours.

Aside from its spectacular scenery and the Canyonlands Park, Moab hadn't received much attention until mountain bikers discovered it a few years ago. In fact, the festival arrived more or less by default when California riders happened to stop there on their way back from Crested Butte.

For more information, write Canyon Country Cyclists, 94 W. 1st North, Moab, UT 84532.

Chequamegon Fat-Tire Festival
Cable, Wisconsin

This two-day bash provides the backdrop for the largest mass-start event in off-road racing, the Chequamegon 40 (say *She-WAMA-gon* and you'll be close). This race follows the same trail as the American Birkebeiner, the biggest Nordic ski race in the country.

Actually, if there's one event that can be defined as friendly competition, this is it. Most riders in the Chequamegon 40 race only once a year, and for many it's debatable whether they're competing or just cruising with a few hundred friends. As the pack streams across the meadows near the start (it usually takes 15 minutes to get everyone going), it seems a mass migration.

Like the Birkie, the 40 cuts through dense forests on the

rolling countryside between Hayward, Wisconsin, and the Telemark Ski Lodge in Cable. Although it's called a trail, the surface is mostly grass and mud. It's usually wide enough to ride two or three abreast. For those who prefer a less-demanding course, there is also a shorter event called the "Short and Fat." The turnout for both is astonishing. At a recent festival, a total of 1,100 riders finished both events.

The Chequamegon Festival is the Midwest's answer to California and Rocky Mountain off-road elitism. What the area lacks in mountain peaks it makes up for with a maze of trails created by the lodge's snow-making machines. This network has spawned another festival favorite, an "orienteering" contest in which participants must follow complicated maps to a series of checkpoints. Since accuracy is as important as speed, this race does not always go to the swift. And naturally, confusion often reigns.

The tone of the entire festival is set by the Chequama Mamas, the bike club that runs the event. Despite its name, the Mamas are not all female, and as a group it rates as one of the least serious clubs in the country. The mission of the Mamas is to have fun—with bikes, without bikes, whatever it takes. The highlight of the postrace banquet, which is attended by hundreds of riders, is the initiation of the newest honorary Mamas. In order to qualify, prospective honorees must scream "Mama!" in front of the assembled multitude. (Believe it or not, it's harder than it sounds.)

For information, write Chequamegon Fat-Tire Festival, Box 267, Telemark Lodge, Cable, WI 54821.

Mammoth Mountain Bike Championships
Mammoth Lakes, California

Although this mega-event is not officially billed as a festival, it incorporates the most important element of one: hordes of mountain bikers gathered for nearly a week.

For several years the California ski resort of Mammoth Mountain has hosted the last big off-road races of the season.

One of the primary attractions here is just watching the sport's best riders compete in every type of fat-tire event, including cross-country, hillclimbs, dual slalom, and observed trials. For those not yet ready to participate at the elite level, there are numerous recreational rides and tours.

For more information, write Mammoth Lakes Championships, Box 24, Mammoth Lakes, CA 93546.

Marin County Fat-Tire Festival
Golden Gate National Seashore, California

Although Marin County is the birthplace of the mountain bike and is generally regarded as a hotbed of the sport, for a number of years there were no major events—competitive or otherwise. Recently, former national off-road champion Jacquie Phelan took matters into her own hands and promoted the first Marin County Fat-Tire Festival. Not at all coincidentally, the gathering of 200 riders on the slopes of Mount Tamalpais served as the backdrop for her wedding to framebuilder Charlie Cunningham.

The wedding is not likely to become an annual event, but the festival will. It's held in the Golden Gate National Seashore area, just north of the Golden Gate Bridge. This large, undeveloped tract of parklands is within spitting distance of San Francisco, where conflicts between mountain bikers and other trail users first surfaced. Phelan gets credit for cutting through the bureaucratic obstacles and generating some of the first positive publicity for mountain bikes in the area in years.

In part, the Marin festival serves as a political statement, a demonstration that mountain bikers can have a great time while working within existing regulations. All cyclists are admonished to stay on the legal routes during the event's numerous recreational rides.

For more information, write: Jacquie Phelan, Box 757, Fairfax, CA 94930.

Other festivals are springing up all across the country. For information, write the National Off-Road Bicycle Association (NORBA), 1750 E. Boulder St., #4, Colorado Springs, CO 80909.

▪33▪ HARD KNOCKS PHOTOGRAPHY

You can capture the beauty of the off-road experience on film without damaging your valuable photographic equipment. Here's how.

An exciting development for mountain bikers is the waterproof 35mm camera. Some models have optional lenses for closer and more distant shooting. Considering the variety of terrain and weather we off-roaders are willing to pedal into, these remarkable cameras seem designed for us. One of their main advantages over 110 cameras is 35mm film. It's considerably larger than 110, so making quality enlargements is much easier. Though these new marvels are still limited compared to standard single-lens-reflex (SLR) cameras, they might be exactly what you need if you can live within their boundaries. They're small, relatively light, and undamaged by water from any source.

The next level is the 35mm SLR camera with interchangeable lenses. With one of these, you can photograph everything from a self-portrait to that toad. Most come equipped with a 50mm lens, which gives you a view through the viewfinder that's about the same as what you see with the naked eye. With any lens, the viewfinder shows you exactly what the lens sees and, thus, what will be on the film. With the Instamatic-type 110s and the shoot-and-point 35mm's, you're looking through a window above the lens, not through it, and must frame your shot with guide lines.

The standard 50mm lens has a fixed focal length. An attractive alternative is a zoom lens, which has a variable focal length. An example is the 35-210mm lens. It gives you the ability to shoot wide angles at 35 mm and pull in distant objects with 210 mm, plus use any focal length between. Another popular choice is a 70-210mm zoom complemented with a "fixed" 28mm wide-angle lens. For bike touring where weight and bulk must be minimized, a single lens such as the 35-210mm is preferable (and it saves lens-changing time). Also avoided is the chance of dust or moisture getting into the camera during lens changes.

There's a trade-off, though. A zoom has a lot of glass between the subject and the film, thus reducing the amount of light reaching it. The less light there is, the slower the film "burns." (Film is a light-sensitive composite of chemicals on which an image burns for as long as the shutter is open.) Decreasing the shutter speed (increasing the length of time the film is exposed to light) is an obvious solution, but the longer the shutter is open, the greater the risk of blurring the image.

A general guideline for hand-held photography is to set the shutter speed equal to the focal lens length. For example, if you're zooming in on a distant subject with the 210mm lens, set the shutter speed no slower than $1/250$ second. For a standard 50mm lens, hand-held photography slower than $1/60$ isn't recommended.

Shooting in low light with a slow shutter speed is possible by placing the camera on a steady surface. For example, you can use a wallet to support the lens while resting the body on a brick wall, a pannier, rocks—anything that's handy. Full-size, portable tripods can be used, though admittedly this is extreme if you aren't shooting professionally. Tripods also are excellent for taking self-portrait action shots. Another option is a small plastic tripod that stands about 4 inches high and has a Velcro strap so it can be attached to a tree limb.

If you want extreme magnification, consider carrying a quality 2X multiplier. Attach it to your zoom lens and jump from 210 to 420 mm. The trade-off, of course, is even less light reaching the film and a minimum shutter speed of $1/500$.

Still another attractive option is a macro lens. Many zooms have a "macro ring." *Macro* means "large." In macro photography, "life-size," "1X," and "1:1" all mean the same thing: the subject will be seen on film the same as it is in life. Half as big would be ½X or 1:2. Macros enable extreme close-ups of flowers and other small subjects. Along the same lines is yet another option for close-up photography, special filters. They're usually sold in sets of three.

Macro photography can be addictive. You'll quickly realize you've been riding over whole worlds of fascinating creatures you never knew existed. Photography, like mountain bikes, can introduce us to much more of the world.

The tricky part of combining 35mm SLR photography

with mountain biking is carrying the gear. Fortunately, a number of manufacturers have anticipated our needs. Flip through the ads of any photography magazine (such as *Outdoor Photography*) and you'll see many options. In fact, there are far too many to go into here. One option is a heavily padded cordura camera bag with a handle on top, which in an instant unzips to become a waistpack with camera and lens compartments. You can carry the camera body with the lens affixed and stow other camera gear in the pouches.

When touring on a road bike, it's nice to have your camera readily available in a handlebar bag (several brands offer padded camera inserts) or resting inside a large camera bag attached to a high-rider front rack. But lenses cannot handle the knocking about that front-rack placement on a mountain bike allows. A handlebar bag disrupts steering on singletracks, so it's equally unsatisfactory. The best off-road placement is inside a pannier with the camera generously padded in its own bag. For photographing fellow riders, keep it handy in a fanny pack. Some riders use chest harnesses to hold the camera tight against their body, but the weight can be bothersome and the camera may become sweaty.

Most camera bags, like panniers, are not waterproof. You can use pannier covers for rain protection. They're superior to the old standby, large "freezer-strength" Ziploc storage bags.

Contrary to what you may think, self-portrait action shots are easy to execute. All you need is a full-height tripod (or tall rock) and any 35mm camera with a 10-second shutter timer. You'll probably take some shots of your back until you get the hang of it. If money is no object, you can buy an infrared or other space-age shutter release that allows you to shoot the picture while riding. Another approach that works well is an inexpensive, lightweight rubber air release bulb and 25 feet of thin rubber hose. With this you can get much farther from the camera before tripping the timer. You then toss the bulb out of the way and hop aboard the bike for the picture.

Smaller aperture (f-stop) settings give greater depth of field, meaning more of the world is in focus. Use small apertures for action self-portraits (most 35mm "automatic" cameras have a manual override to allow this) to avoid pedaling out of focus range.

For these action shots, try a full-length tripod with flip-lock legs. It's surprisingly light. A cordura bag protects it from the weather, and you can carry it like a sleeping bag across the rack. In good weather you can keep it handy for instant access. You may not understand why any biker would want to bother with a tripod until you've given one a try. It's very helpful when the light is low.

No technique will help if your film isn't up to par. The intense heat that can occur inside panniers may ruin color film. While black-and-white handles heat well, few cyclists use it; everyone wants color. Kodachrome is basically a black-and-white film until processing, when coloration "couplers" are introduced. If you want to shoot slides in hot weather, you would do well to use Kodachrome in place of Ektachrome. Besides, magazines generally prefer Kodachrome, and who's to say you won't snap a cover shot your next time out?

34 WINTER CARE

Cold-weather riding can be a blast, but it requires special precautions. Your body is a vehicle for your brain to have fun. The brain doesn't enjoy being cold. It's a matter of survival, really, because as soon as its temperature sinks a couple of degrees, it begins to lose control. With no one in charge, your body can get into serious trouble.

When the temperature starts to drop, the brain's first response is to draw blood away from the cold skin. If blood becomes chilled near the surface, it returns to the core of the brain too cold. The brain starts to feel a draft. Bundling the head helps. The brain becomes more willing to allow warm blood to flow elsewhere, for instance to cold feet.

Here are some other tips for safe riding in cold weather:

1. Avoid cramming a second pair of socks into the same size cycling shoes you wore last summer. Compressing your feet reduces circulation. Winter shoes should be at least one size larger. If you use toe straps, remember to loosen these, too.

2. Don't wear cotton socks under wool socks. Cotton caresses while wool scratches, but it also collects the moisture your feet continually produce. If your skin hates anything more than compression, it's wetness. The moisture evaporates, reducing the temperature of the skin in chilling leaps.

A synthetic sock liner is comfy and allows the moisture to migrate away from your feet and into the wool. Toes stay drier, thus warmer. Remember that we're heat-producing units, and clothing that protects us from heat loss is the clothing we should wear.

Photograph 5-2. When you dress correctly for cold weather, mountain biking becomes a year-round sport.

In fact, we make more heat than we can use, so we need to lose exactly the right amount to maintain a normal, healthy temperature in our core.

Four mechanisms exist for shedding excess warmth:

- Convection. Warmth escapes by air movement, especially the kind we create by riding a bike.
- Conduction. When we touch something cold, heat is drawn from us to the object.

- Evaporation. This cools our entire body and accounts for the heat lost in puffs of vapor when we breathe on a cold day.
- Radiation. Heat constantly escapes into the environment this way.

Normally, everything's fine as long as we don't give off more heat than we produce. So dress in layers: a windproof outer shell over bulky insulating clothing over a soft, nonabsorbent covering next to the skin to wick away the moisture.

3. Wear your clothing correctly. The best clothing can still fail to keep us warm if we wear it incorrectly. We know we're going to sweat when we increase our activity, so it's best to take off outer layers before they get soggy. As soon as you stop, add layers back before you get chilled. Trap the heat you've made so you don't have to produce more.

4. Drink as much as or more than you would during summer. In winter, a low fluid level means a low blood volume, which in turn means a predisposition to the problems caused by cold. Also, adequate water intake will reduce the risk of frostbite and prevent fatigue caused by dehydration.

You need to drink 3 to 4 quarts every day. But don't wait until thirst nags you. Cold blunts the thirst response. Besides, feeling thirsty is a sign that your personal water table already is low. Drink because you know you should, not because you're thirsty.

5. Save the alcohol until you're home by the fire. Booze may make you feel warmer, but it actually increases your body's ability to lose heat. You can suffer a tremendous loss of warmth without realizing it. Minutes after imbibing, your brain is less concerned about your welfare. And alcohol causes an urge to release fluid, not retain it. All things considered, alcohol and cold are an unhealthful mix.

6. Recognize the signs of too much cold. The first sign is a subtle loss of thought processes. When the brain cools, the body responds to its commands sluggishly and carelessly. Fine motor skills go next. It becomes difficult to tie your shoes or zip your parka. The brain knows what the hand should be doing, but can't seem to get the message there. Then an involuntary survival response kicks in: shivering. Even though this "exercise" makes heat, the core temperature drops rapidly. It's important to get warm and dry.

These tips will help you avoid the risks of winter off-road riding. Use them and you'll be safe and healthy as you enjoy this great time of year to be on a mountain bike.

35 WEIGHT WORKOUTS

There's no argument that riding a mountain bike requires more upper-body strength than riding a road bike, but off-roaders have lagged behind in making weight training part of their fitness program. It's time to change this.

Before we outline a simple but effective program you can follow at home, let's see how weight training can increase your cycling performance and safety whether you're a racer or recreational rider.

Upper-Body Strength

Newcomers to mountain biking are often shocked at the demands the sport places on their upper body. Pulling the front wheel over logs, hanging on during rough downhills, and carrying the bike up unridable hills require an upper body that doesn't just go along for the ride. As pro racer David Turner notes, "Mountain biking places a big stress on your upper body, a constant vibrational pounding." Adds multinational champ Joe Murray, "Road riders will start riding off-road and say their upper bodies get real sore."

Of course, you gain some strength from riding, so why not just head for the hills and forget the iron therapy? As Turner explains, "You get strong [on the bike] only through a limited range of motion." But weight training works your muscles through their full range. Murray adds, "Weights keep your muscle tone up in winter, so it's easier to get your cardiovascular fitness back when you start riding again." If your winters are too snowy to ride consistently, the weight room will take up the slack.

Surprisingly, a strong upper body will also make you faster. According to Turner, "Speeds in mountain bike racing are increasing steadily in part because bike-handling skills are getting better. Racers are taking more aggressive lines. And weight training allows you to take a tougher line and get away with it."

Injury Prevention

A strong upper body also helps prevent injuries when you crash. Strengthening the shoulder girdle protects your vulnerable collarbones, but neck and upper back exercises are even more important. After all, a good helmet will protect your skull in an over-the-bar crash, but this won't matter much if your neck is broken. A resistance training program can easily include exercises to strengthen this vital area. Wrestlers' bridges are excellent, as are workouts on the various neck machines at a club. Also, Turner advocates dumbbell shrugs to work the trapezius muscles that connect the neck to the shoulder girdle.

Also important is your midsection. Abdominal muscles aren't worked when you ride, but strong abs are vital; they support and align your back. Murray suggests "doing a lot of abdominal stuff because when you ride you stretch out the lower back." Do abdominal curls to isolate your abdominals rather than straight-leg sit-ups that tend to aggravate back problems.

Power Development

If you grind to a halt on hills or have trouble plowing through mud and sand, you need more power. And weight training is the fastest way to get crank-cracking power in a hurry. Start with a varied lower-body weight program. In Turner's view, "Calf raises, hamstring curls, and leg extensions are good because they exercise the muscles through a full range of motion—you use the muscles more than in the pedaling motion." Squats and leg presses are also excellent.

For hard-core riders, Turner suggests an off-season combination of weights, along with power work on the bike. "Pick a short hill with unlimited traction," he advises. "Use a heavy bike and do short sprints [20 to 30 seconds] up the hill. Concentrate on form and pulling through. Get serious about it—hammer up, coast down, get a full rest, then do it again. Then go into the gym and finish breaking down your legs with full-range weight exercises."

Equipment

Some riders, like Murray and Turner, join a health club in the winter. Many clubs sell short memberships at a reduced rate. Clubs offer the advantages of a wide selection of equipment, other people to shame or encourage you into training, and a powerful motivation to show up several days a week (you'd better go because you paid your money). Disadvantages? Expense, wasted time commuting to the club, limited hours, and often the inconvenience of waiting in line for equipment.

As a result, many riders use a simple home gym. For less than the cost of a three-month club membership you can acquire the basics: a pull-up bar, a 110-pound weight set, and a bench. You won't need more weight for cycling fitness, and fancy machines, while they make exercising high tech, really aren't necessary. You'll also need an open area of at least 8×8 feet with enough ceiling clearance to get the barbell overhead. Basements and family rooms are popular; apartment living rooms or garages work in a pinch.

If you have more room and a bigger budget, add two 25-pound plates and a bench that adjusts for incline presses and has a leg curl/extension attachment.

Lifting Lingo

Before we look at specific programs, here are some useful weight training terms. In addition, the illustrations on pages 114 to 117 show how to do the recommended exercises.

Lifters talk about sets and reps. A rep is one repetition of an exercise movement. A set is a predetermined number of reps. Lifters use shorthand to record their workouts in a diary. If you do three sets of ten repetitions, it's denoted as 3×10.

Cyclists don't need to lift enormous amounts or build large muscles. You want strength, flexibility, and endurance, so leave the heavy weights for the power lifters. Start with a weight light enough to permit at least 15 reps in good form without straining.

Illustration 5-1. Bent Row: With your knees bent and back straight, pull the barbell up to your chest, then lower slowly.

Illustration 5-2. Shoulder Shrug: Roll your shoulders forward and upward as far as possible, then pause and lower slowly.

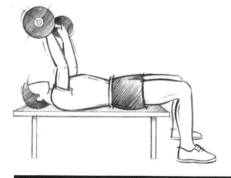

Illustration 5-3. Bench Press: While keeping your back flat against the bench, push the barbell to full extension, then lower slowly.

Never lift without a complete warm-up. Run, ride an indoor trainer, stretch, do calisthenics, play basketball—anything to break a sweat and get the muscles loose. Weight training won't cause injuries if done properly, and a safe workout begins with a solid warm-up.

Circuit training is a popular way to work out with weights. You move through a series of 10 to 15 exercises, doing repetitions of each for 20 seconds, then resting for 20 seconds before going to the next. Work up to three trips through the circuit. Use extremely light weights so you aren't gasping and losing form by the end of the workout.

A maintenance program is done during the riding season so you won't lose the hard-won strength you gained in winter. One or two workouts a week is sufficient. You don't even need weights—just do pull-ups, push-ups, curls, and neck bridges for 10 to 15 minutes after a ride.

Illustration 5-4. Upright Row: Pull the barbell to the top of your chest, then lower slowly. Keep the bar close to your body.

Illustration 5-5. Squat: With your back straight and the barbell on your shoulders, slowly squat until your thighs are parallel to the floor, then stand up.

Illustration 5-6. Neck Bridge: Using a pad for your head, arch your back and roll fore and aft.

Illustration 5-7. Press: With your hands shoulder-width apart, push the barbell overhead until your arms are fully extended, then lower slowly.

Periodization means dividing your training schedule into short cycles to avoid burnout. Let's say you want to lift seriously in January, February, and March. In January, do a general program of low weights, high reps, and include exercises for all the muscle groups. This program breaks you in gradually, preparing your body for the higher intensities to come. In February, go for power with more weight, increased sets, and fewer reps. Do fewer exercises, too, and involve more of the body at once—do cleans rather than upright rows, for instance. In March, prepare your body for the fast-paced demands of cycling with circuit training.

Here's a sample off-season lifting program designed to get you in top shape by spring.

Illustration 5-8. Abdominal Curl: With your knees well bent, curl forward until your shoulders are 6 to 12 inches off the floor. Hold, then lower slowly.

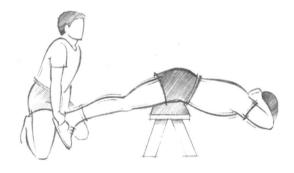

Illustration 5-9. Back Extension: With your torso hanging over a padded bench, straighten your back until your body is horizontal, then lower slowly.

January: General Conditioning

Monday: Warm up for 20 minutes, then do one to three sets of 10 to 25 reps of pull-ups, curls, presses, neck bridges, upright rows, squats, push-ups, and calf raises. Use light weights and keep your intensity low. Concentrate on good form.

Wednesday: Same as Monday, but change the exercises to push-ups, bent rows, bench presses, presses behind the neck, back extensions, jump squats, curls, and neck bridges.

Friday: Same as Monday.

February: Power Development

Monday: Warm up for 20 minutes, then do three to five sets of 10 to 15 reps of cleans, presses, squats, calf raises, curls, and neck bridges.
Wednesday: Same as Monday, but change the exercises to bench presses, bent rows, step-ups onto a bench, shoulder shrugs, curls, and neck bridges.
Friday: Same as Monday.

March: Circuit Training

Monday: Warm up for 20 minutes, then do a circuit consisting of pull-ups, push-ups, neck bridges, squats, presses, upright rows, curls, calf raises, cleans, running in place, bench presses, bent rows, and shoulder shrugs.
Thursday: Same as Monday.

April

As the weather improves and you begin riding more frequently, continue lifting twice a week. Do circuit training one day and take your choice of workouts on the other.

May

Once or twice a week, do the maintenance program outlined above. Continue each month until the return of winter curtails your riding, then begin another indoor program of general conditioning as just outlined.

Tips to Remember

1. Use light weights!
2. Always maintain proper form. Supplement this infor-

mation with an illustrated weight training book or the advice of a professional strength coach at your local club or school.

3. You're welcome to substitute your favorite exercises for those listed.

4. Vary your routine or skip a workout if you start to feel stale.

5. Train with a partner—it makes weight lifting safer, more fun, and you can encourage each other.

6. On days you don't lift, do an aerobic workout such as cycling (if possible), running, hiking, cross-country skiing, riding on a resistance trainer, and so on.

7. Finally, realize that a strength building program doesn't have to include formal weight training to be effective. Other vigorous activities can work. Top racer Ned Overend says, "I just do pull-ups, sit-ups, push-ups, and work on my abdominals." And elite racer Lisa Muhich takes the minimalist approach: "I don't feel I need to lift in the off-season. I do rock climbing and work around the yard. It's my body type—I don't care to develop any more muscle than I already have."

But if you've noticed your forearms fatiguing before your quads, or if you've been plagued with nagging muscle strains, give weight training a try this winter. You'll become stronger, more resilient, and faster than you were before.

◨ Credits

The information in this book is drawn from these articles in *Bicycling* and *Mountain Bike* magazines.

"Go Ahead, Get Dirty" Fred Matheny, "Go Ahead, Get Dirty," *Bicycling,* May 1987.

"Buying a Mountain Bike" John Kukoda, "Everything You Always Wanted to Know. . ." *Bicycling,* May 1987.

"Fat-Tire Therapy" Hank Barlow, "Fat-Tire Therapy," *Mountain Bike,* May/June 1988.

"Dirty Dressing" Hank Barlow, "Dirty Dressing," *Mountain Bike,* September/October 1989.

"Tool Talk" Gregg Morin, "Tool Talk," *Mountain Bike,* March/April 1988.

"Care and Cleaning" Don Cuerdon and Gary Fisher, "The Care and Cleaning of an ATB," *Bicycling,* May 1987.

"Fear Not" Ellen J. Meyers, Ph.D., "Fear Not," *Mountain Bike,* September/October 1989.

"Eight Skill Builders" Don Cuerdon, "Skill Builders," *Bicycling,* November 1988.

"Using Your Eyes" Hank Barlow, "The Eyes Have It," *Mountain Bike,* July/August 1989.

"Biking the Line" Hank Barlow, "Biking the Line," *Mountain Bike,* September/October 1988.

"Going Up?" Hank Barlow, "Going Up?" *Mountain Bike,* January/February 1989.

"Starting on a Hill" Hank Barlow, "Starting on a Hill," *Mountain Bike,* January/February 1988.

"Maximum Traction" John N. Olsen, "Maximum Traction," *Bicycling,* May 1988.

"Downshifting" Hank Barlow, "Update on Downshifting," *Mountain Bike,* May/June 1988.

"Giving Your Bike a Ride" Hank Barlow, "How to Give Your Bike a Ride," *Mountain Bike,* March/April 1988.

"Biking While Loaded" Hank Barlow, "Biking While Loaded," *Mountain Bike,* July/August 1988.

"Creek Crossings" Bob Ward, "Take the Plunge," *Mountain Bike,* March/April 1989.

"Log Jumping" Hank Barlow, "Log Jumping," *Mountain Bike,* May/June 1989.

"The Bunny Hop" Hank Barlow, "The Bunny Hop," *Mountain Bike,* September/October 1989.

"Advanced Trail Techniques" John Lehrer, "Advanced Trail Techniques," *Bicycling,* May 1987.

"Practicing at Home" John Lehrer, "Homework," *Bicycling,* May 1987.

"Weather Awareness" Gary Sprung, "Weather Awareness," *Mountain Bike,* July/August 1989.

"Map Reading" Dennis Coello, "Map Reading," *Mountain Bike,* July/August 1989.

"Compass Navigation" Dennis Coello, "Compass Navigation," *Mountain Bike,* July/August 1989.

"Nutritional Energy" Buck Tilton, "Nutritional Energy," *Mountain Bike,* July/August 1989.

"Your Portable Hospital" Gary Sprung, "Your Portable Hospital," *Mountain Bike,* May/June 1988.

"Treating Eye Injuries" Buck Tilton, "Here's Mud in Your Eye," *Mountain Bike,* September/October 1988.

"Dealing with Head Injuries" Buck Tilton, "Head Cases," *Mountain Bike,* January/February 1989.

"Treating Sprains and Strains" Buck Tilton, "Sprains and Strains," *Mountain Bike,* March/April 1989.

"Water in the Wild" Buck Tilton, "Water in the Wild," *Mountain Bike,* May/June 1989.

"Your First Mountain Bike Race" Charles Kelly, "Your First Mountain Bike Race," *Mountain Bike,* May/June 1989.

"Mountain Bike Festivals" Charles Kelly, "Fat Fests," *Bicycling,* June 1989.

"Hard Knocks Photography" Dennis Coello, "Hard Knocks Photography," *Mountain Bike,* January/February 1988.

"Winter Care" Buck Tilton, "Wintercare," *Mountain Bike,* November/December 1988.

"Weight Workouts" Fred Matheny, "Weighting for You," *Mountain Bike,* January/February 1989.

Photographs and Illustrations

Scott Markewitz: photo 2-1; Bob Ward: photo 2-2; Stan Green: photos 2-3, 2-4, 2-5; Carl Yarbrough: photo 2-6; Rodale Stock Images: photo 4-1; J. Michael Wyatt: photo 4-2; Nathan Bilow: photo 5-1; Egidio: photo 5-2.

Catherine L. Reed: illustration 1-1; Kathi Ember: illustrations 5-1, 5-2, 5-3, 5-4, 5-5, 5-6, 5-7, 5-8, 5-9.

Rodale Press, Inc., publishes BICYCLING, America's leading cycling magazine. For information on how to order your subscription, write to BICYCLING, Emmaus, PA 18098.